AS TIME GOES BY

DEREK TAYLOR

FABER & FABER

First published in 1973 by Davis-Poynter Ltd
This edition first published in the UK in 2018
by Faber & Faber Ltd, Bloomsbury House,
74–77 Great Russell Street, London WC1B 3DA

First published in the USA in 2018

Typeset by Reality Premedia Services Pvt. Ltd.
Printed and bound in the UK by CPI Group (UK) Ltd, Croydon CR0 4YY

A CIP record for this book
is available from the British Library

ISBN 978–0–571–34266–2

FSC
www.fsc.org
MIX
Paper from
responsible sources
FSC® C020471

10 9 8 7 6 5 4 3 2

This book was written for – and because of –
Joan, Annabel, Dominic, Vanessa, Victoria,
Gerard and Timothy. Without them I would be
a decrepit old fool. With them, I am indeed
a fortunate young man.

Contents

A new introduction
by Jon Savage

'Did it happen, all of it, or was it a dream?'
Derek Taylor, *As Time Goes By*, Chapter 19

The world first focused on Derek Taylor in 1964, when he wrote the sleeve note to the multi-million-selling *Beatles for Sale* album. The previous three Beatles albums all had notes on the back but these were a definite step up – a winning mixture of hype, acute analysis and sharp humour: 'The young men themselves aren't for sale. Money, noisy though it is, doesn't talk that loud. But you can buy this album – you probably have, unless you're just browsing, in which case don't leave any dirty thumbprints on the sleeve!'

Most of all, Derek Taylor understood that the Beatles were not a transitory phenomenon but would last into the twenty-first century: 'When, in a generation or so, a radio-active, cigar-smoking child, picnicking on Saturn, asks you what the Beatle affair was all about – "Did you actually know them?" – don't try to explain all about the long hair and the screams! Just play the child a few tracks from this album and he'll probably understand what it was all about. The kids of AD 2000 will draw from the music much the same sense of well-being and warmth as we do today.'

1

Between 1964 and 1970, Derek Taylor was a Beatle intimate. Beginning as an observer and a fan, he became, in turn, their press officer and travelling companion; their supplicant; their friend; their colleague in the utopian visions of Apple; and, finally, the keeper of the flame just as it was being, albeit temporarily, extinguished. Apart from Brian Epstein – whose absolute faith would never be swayed and was fully repaid – he was the only Beatle insider who was able to clearly communicate a wider perspective on the events that they were living through.

Born in May 1932, Taylor was a decade or so older than the four Beatles and this, plus his old-school journalistic training, gave him the toughness and the distance to survive being in the centre of the storm – and then the ability to write beautifully about the experience. He was, above all, a proselytiser, with a sure sense of the Beatles' importance, the intricacies of their interpersonal relationships, and the precise nature of their myth as it was in the process of construction. Having had his life changed, he wanted others to share the experience.

At the same time, he was not a Beatle. He was at first Brian Epstein's personal assistant at NEMS, and then the Beatles' employee – as, in a couple of terse exchanges reproduced in this book, he was occasionally reminded. Yet he was more than that. In 1964, he gave the job of Beatle press officer a sense of class that made him a mini-celebrity in the eyes of the Brit-hungry American media. During 1968 and 1969 he was the go-to person at Apple – a vital function which he executed in a bedazzling torrent of words.

Derek could charm the hind legs off a horse, and, as a poacher-turned-gamekeeper, understood exactly how the different sections of the press worked at any given time. His chapter 'Of a day in 1968' was written 'while still fresh', and in four long paragraphs, it captures the mad immediacy of having to deal with at least thirty demanding journalists from around the world at the same time. It's his job to placate the voracious beast and, by the end of the day, he doesn't know who he is: 'I must be crazy. I am crazy. And so are you. And so are they. So it's OK.'

Derek Taylor was that rare beast: a Fleet Street man who left its brotherhood and then criticised its inner workings. As he writes, 'Your newspaper reporter lives in a strange and frightening world, oversimplified by the need to write in baby-talk, overcomplicated because the reporter is never told the whole truth.' He cites a dozen or so hoary cliches ('a world where . . . judges lash rapists and governments are flayed by the opposition') before concluding: 'For a week or two, it is OK, even exciting. After fifteen years, which is how long I lived in it, it becomes a pain.'

At the time when pop was just for the young, incomprehensible to adults, he crossed over the generational divide and never even thought about coming back. As he writes in Chapter 18 about the year 1969 (when he turned thirty-seven), 'Me, I think the grownups are daft. They are Martians, sitting on the trains with their erections hidden under their *Evening Standards*. I hate them.' He swapped professional cynicism for belief and wonder – an unforgivable sin in some eyes, but then he understood history.

How did this happen? Derek Taylor was from Merseyside – West Kirby on the Wirral if we are being specific – and he had a deep knowledge and respect for the city over the water.

3

His world was formed in postwar austerity: dressing like your parents, the Festival of Britain, two years of National Service. In this memoir, he writes about the famous people he met in his early days on the *Hoylake and West Kirby Advertiser*, glimmers of postwar glamour: Richard Attenborough, Danny Kaye – thus far, thus early 1950s.

In 1955, he joined the *Liverpool Echo* and *Daily Post*, before moving to the expiring *Sunday Dispatch* and then onto the *Daily Express* in 1962. His conversion came in late May 1963, when he went with his wife Joan to review the Beatles/Roy Orbison package tour in Manchester: 'The Liverpool sound came to Manchester last night,' he wrote in the paper that night, 'and I thought it was magnificent . . . Indecipherable, meaningless nonsense, of course, but as beneficial and invigorating as a week on the bench of the pierhead overlooking the Mersey.'

His later recollections in *Fifty Years Adrift* went further than his contemporary tabloid-ese: 'It has always seemed to me that the true essence of the Beatles is to be found distilled in "From Me to You". Boy–girl love song it may have been, but it was also a universal offering, spelled out with Liverpool directness and warmth and picked up by a whole generation including, from that night on, Joan and me. Though maybe at the "wrong" end of that generation, we were nevertheless open thereafter to the possibilities of being truly young in heart.'

A few weeks later, Taylor interviewed Epstein for the *Express*: commissioned, as he later remembered, to write a feature about 'the man behind the Beatles. Svengali stuff. I did this interview with this amazing man, with his monogrammed shirt and his buckle shoes, and we got on awfully well, considering what a front he had. He was awfully remote. People hadn't been asking anything for very long. So he did like the interview, but also had this kind of sniffy front, but that didn't fool me, cos I was from Liverpool.'

Out of this meeting came a rapport that resulted in Taylor being hired to ghost Epstein's memoir: 'In the first lunch hour, he said, I'm going to have to tell you now, did you know I was queer? No, I said, I didn't. Well, he said, I am, and if we're going to do this book I'm going to have to stop buggering about, saying I was with this girl, when I was with a boy. Does that make any difference? No, I said, it does not make any difference, it'll make it a lot easier, so you mustn't worry any more, difficult as it may be to convince you perhaps, but I won't ever let you down.'

Trust thus established, Taylor became Epstein's personal assistant at NEMS and in short order, the Beatles' press officer. He left Fleet Street without a thought, as he writes in this book: 'I had been working for the *Daily Express* but you can only do that for so long without going mad'. Packed off on the group's world tour of 1964, he was thrust into close proximity with the four Beatles and their two assistants, Neil Aspinall and Mal Evans, while witnessing wild scenes in Australia, America and New Zealand – Beatlemania at its very height.

Some of the flavour of the madness can be gauged in his quotes from Al Aronowitz's August 1964 cover story for the *Saturday Evening Post*:

'It's incredible, absolutely incredible', says Derek Taylor, the Beatles' press officer. 'Here are these four boys from Liverpool. They're rude, they're profane, they're vulgar

5

and they've taken over the world. It's as if they'd founded a new religion. They're completely anti-Christ. I mean, I'm anti-Christ as well, but they're so anti-Christ they shock me, which isn't an easy thing. But I'm obsessed with them. Isn't everybody? I'm obsessed with their honesty. And the people who like them most are the people who should be outraged most. In Australia, for example, each time we'd arrived at an airport, it was as if De Gaulle had landed, or better yet, the Messiah. The routes were lined solid, cripples threw away their sticks, sick people rushed up to the car as if a touch from one of the boys would make them well again, old women stood watching with their grandchildren, and as we'd pass by, I could see the look on their faces. It was as if some saviour had arrived and all these people were happy and relieved, as if things somehow were going to be better now.'

Taylor was a keen observer, and like many in close proximity to fame but not suffering its burden, he was ideally placed to see how it distorted everyone who came within its orbit. He saw the distinction between what the group sang about – 'as John Lennon said, "Our songs were always about peace and freedom and love"' – and the attitudes of fans and fame groupies: a racist taxi driver and his son, a 'hard as hell' mayor's wife who was disgusted by these 'four long-haired louts from nowhere' but still wanted to meet them.

Living on a diet of brandy and a morning ritual of 'two small yellow dexedrine tablets', Taylor climaxed the tour in an explosive argument with Brian Epstein. Although the regrets soon flowed, it was the end of his working relationship with NEMS. After working out his notice, he moved with Joan and four young children to Hollywood where his stint as PR to the biggest group in the world brought him many clients: Paul Revere and the Raiders, the Beau Brummels, Captain Beefheart, the Beach Boys and, for a brief moment, the Doors.

His real love, however, was the Byrds: 'We worshipped the Byrds very much, Joan and I, and there has never been anything to touch us with quite so much magic as the first line-up singing their hits on Sunset Boulevard in the mid-sixties.' In summer 1965, Taylor returned to the UK as PA for the Byrds on their first British tour: a difficult trip with hostile press notices and chaotic shows – 'all the time, aggro, and panic' as he wrote. In their service he 'became a real publicist, finding energies and concentration and a shameless fluency I had never known before'.

Derek's stint in Los Angeles was a high-wire act of hustling, publicising and writing for the expanding pop press, *Tiger Beat, Teen, Disc and Music Echo*: 'Clean, honest opinions and views made up the bulk of it and in this way I was able to drop in the name of clients who weren't making any waves with their music.' Such a thing was common in the music industry of the time but still, there was role strain: was he PR, journalist, trend-setter or opinion-former? All four at once, no doubt. However there were situations which even his native wit couldn't finesse.

One of the delights of *As Time Goes By* is the way in which Taylor is able to tell stories against himself, to acknowledge his mistakes. It is this honesty that makes him a reliable narrator in the midst of mirrors and myth. Early in his Hollywood days, for instance, he was asked by his main sponsor, Bob Eubanks, to go out to the Bahamas to buttonhole his former clients as they were filming *Help!*: 'Bob's idea was that I would use my relationship with them, my friendship even, and get interviews which would be unique.'

The encounters were excruciating. Taylor records Paul McCartney's reaction: '"Bloody hell," he said when he saw me. "Bloody hell, Derek. You with a tape-recorder asking us questions?" Oh yes, me with a tape-recorder. The thing was what was the thing I was? Their friend or a journalist or their ex-publicist Brian Epstein's ex-personal assistant or a puppet of Bob Eubanks or a man in search of a career in American radio or what? The answer is I didn't think there was any choice.' The Beatles relented, and after a few sticky moments, the matter was forgotten.

In late 1966, Taylor found himself in the epicentre of the emerging American counterculture when the Byrds' manager Jim Dickson started an organisation called CAFF – Community Action for Fact and Freedom – to help the young people caught up in the Sunset Strip Riots in Los Angeles that year. This occurred because realtors and restaurant owners on the Strip felt that the masses of teenagers thronging the sidewalks hurt their trade and insisted that police enforce a curfew held over from the middle of the Second World War.

The battles were savage in what Derek called 'the whole rotten issue of the Old v the Young', and were repeated for several weekends in November and December 1966. He went down to the demonstration and was shocked at the violence: 'I saw my first police "flying wedge" on Sunset Boulevard, saw how professional cops can always crush amateur freedomniks if they have a mind to, saw a sheriff's deputy spit on

8

a woman, saw Peter Fonda in handcuffs, saw how bad things could be before they got worse, like now.'

Nevertheless, California was where it was at after the demise of Swinging London. During the next few months, Taylor wrote about events on the West Coast in his influential *Disc and Music Echo* column, 'Our Man in America'. As he wrote in March 1967, 'Beards and jeans and lace cloaks, waist-length hair, tranquillity and underground literature – these will be the visual symbols of the "Love-In". But beneath this lies a yearning for an end to America's right-wingery, grey-conformity and war-involvement. Thank you.'

Thus radicalised, Taylor got involved as press officer for the Monterey Pop Festival – the one event that, even more than January's Human Be-In, announced the Summer of Love and the West Coast as the pop epicentre. The Beatles were not present, but their antennae were highly tuned: shortly after the festival, Derek and Joan Taylor were invited to a party at Brian Epstein's house in Sussex, where they were fully admitted back into the fold. They also had their first exposure to LSD.

'We saw wonderful things,' Taylor remembered in the interviews for *Anthology*, 'and we changed. We became hippies really, and the Beatles changed a lot from being rather charming but quite worldly-wise pop stars into being extremely nice, gently huggable souls. They were really very sweet in 1967 and we believed we were going to make everything very beautiful, that it was going to be a wonderful world. Now the idea of going back to England from California after having had three good years there – I thought this was it – this was the Holy Land.'

The party was the prelude to Taylor being invited back to the UK in early 1968 to be press officer at the newly instituted Apple offices – at first in Wigmore Street, and then in Savile Row. Envisioned in the communal summer of 1967, Apple was to be an organisation that would encompass film, music, retail and electronics – managed and staffed by the four most famous musicians on the planet and their hand-picked assistants. The slow unravelling of this utopian premise – 'this promise to save mankind' as Taylor called it – is the principal focus of this book.

As Time Goes By was begun in 1968 when Derek Taylor got a contract with the American publisher Prentice-Hall: no doubt his Beatles connection was thought sales-worthy. However he found writing the projected book difficult: fully embroiled in the daily business of Apple, he had neither the time nor the distance necessary to complete the contract. But he kept notes as he was going along, and these capture the immediacy of events as they came thick and fast during 1968, 1969 and 1970.

During those years, Apple released four extremely successful albums by the Beatles, nurtured the career of Mary Hopkin, and released fascinating records by James Taylor, Badfinger and John Taverner among others. It changed the idea of what the relationship between a record company and an artist could be. At the same time, the Beatles' lives were in turmoil with drug busts, changes of partners, provocative happenings, business wrangles and the prolonged rumours of division and demise.

During those years, Apple became a tabloid fixture, and that's what Derek Taylor had to deal with on a daily basis

– as well as the constant stream of supplicants hoping to catch some Beatle magic. As he remembered in the tapes for the *Anthology* film: 'So I'm sitting there in a white wicker chair, formerly owned by Claudine Longet which I brought over from A&M Records, full of hubris and ambition and drink and madness as the dispenser of the wisdom, the cups of tea and what is it you guys want. And then once again these hordes were pouncing on me.

'It wasn't all madness,' he remembered. 'It was just that you couldn't keep the madness out, the madness came in with the sensible stuff.' This book was an early source for many of the stories that have since become familiar: the arrival of Hells Angels at Apple's front door in December 1968, the business wrangles with publisher Dick James, the introduction of Allen Klein into Beatle business, the drug busts and the endless business and personality struggles. By mid-1969 it was becoming, as he wrote, 'a wasteland, a minefield'.

'We Appled for hours,' Taylor describes an evening at this time: 'Appling being the inexhaustible pastime of putting our house to rights in theory without having the power to do it in practice. It is like playing Monopoly, and like Monopoly, it can be played by anyone, and often is. Apple staff don't enjoy playing it with non-Applers, however: they ask too many questions and they talk after they have left. God knows to whom, but that they talk is clear from our clippings service.'

If 1969 was 'a terrible year' at Apple, then 1970 saw the end of Taylor's time. In April, he was the person to whom journalists came seeking quotes about Paul McCartney's statement that the Beatles would not work together again. He was the public face of the split, which he finessed with this fine statement: 'Spring is here and Leeds play Chelsea tomorrow and Ringo and John and George and Paul are alive and well and living in hope. The world is still spinning and so are we and so are you. When the spinning stops, that'll be the time to worry. Not before.'

'The fun stopped when there was very little to do,' Taylor remembered in *Anthology*; 'George said go home and write a book, which was *As Time Goes By*. And I went home and that was 1970 and had a very nice time at home with Joan and it was a very nice year, a beautiful summer, and "Let It Be" came out. The Beatles had broken up, there was really no press officering to do in Apple, not really, and I left on New Year's Eve 1970, joined Warner Brothers the following morning.'

Like many of those closely involved with the Beatles, Taylor found their absence hard: 'There are about eighty things wrong with working for the Beatles and one of them is that there aren't any Beatles any more and another is that one forgets who one is, whoever one may be; the experience of working for the Beatles has affected all of us in different ways, but affected us it has and forever; come what may we will never be the same.' As he concluded in typical Derek style: 'For myself, I have no complaints.'

As Time Goes By was first published in 1973, around the same time as Richard DiLello's *The Longest Cocktail Party* (about which Taylor is generous in Chapter 12 here). The rancorous split had seen the Beatles' reputation reach a low ebb, but these two books – in their different ways – helped to restate the group's importance and to remind the reader of what had been lost. In tandem with the two massively successful *1962–66* and *1967–70* albums, the Beatles were revived for successive generations.

This is a wise and witty account, written by an insider who appreciated insiders – the behind-the-scenes people who make the music and entertainment industry run. Derek Taylor was quite capable of smoke and mirrors himself but here he tells the truth as he sees it – not just about the Beatles and Apple but about himself. It's this self-knowledge that brings you up short: acknowledging his complicity in the splendours and the follies that saturate pop and are thus amplified to the sound of infinity in the story of the biggest twentieth-century entertainment phenomenon.

Nevertheless, *As Time Goes By* has the quality of an exorcism – of something that needed to be written for deeper reasons than just telling a good story (although that is reason enough). It would not be the last time that Derek wrote about the Beatles – he took another comprehensive crack at it with *Fifty Years Adrift*, published in 1984 – but this has all the crackling energy of a first book. At once angry and confused, fluent and blunt, erudite and crude, these twenty-six chapters have all the urgency of a burden shared and thus lifted.

1 / About today written today

This book was started in the sixties somewhere, as random notes. As a book it began in 1968 when I worked for the Beatles and Apple in London. I began it because Joan and also Fred Roos, a Hollywood casting director, said I should. They said, 'You should write a book.'

I said, 'I can't write a book. I would never finish it.' But Fred is a casting director. He gives people roles. So he introduced me to Mitchell Hamilburger, a literary agent in Los Angeles who offered me assistance from Sylva Romano who worked for him. Sylva asked me would I write a book. 'Oh, yes, OK,' I said.

Sylva fixed me with the publishers Prentice-Hall who gave me $2,500 which locked me into a contract. So, about four years ago, I began it. They were hard times then, you know. Apple days of dreaming and screaming for a way out of the confusion.

In 1970, three Prentice-Hall editors later, the book was nowhere near finished. George Harrison sent me home from Apple and gave me six months to finish the damn thing. One day Prentice-Hall wrote to Sylva and said they insisted on seeing some words from me. I sent them what I had. They wrote to Sylva again and said something like, 'This is not a book, and this which is not a book is written by a man who

15

doesn't want to write a book.' They asked for the return of their advance. Asked? Demanded.

Thank God, said I, and stopped writing. Joan – who lives with me as my wife, and who is the mother of our six children – said, 'It's important you should write this book. People will want to read it.' Really I believed her. She has never lied to me. So, for her, I carried on. A few pages here and a few words there and sometimes a piece long enough to be called a chapter. Barely.

It was very easy sometimes and sometimes it was very difficult. When it was easy I enjoyed doing it. When it was difficult I didn't enjoy doing it. I figured that it was much the same with everyone. Then it became a real drag and I stopped. Lazy. Idle. Can do good work if he tries. Sylva was very good. She carried on looking for a new publisher. She found Straight Arrow Books, who published *Rolling Stone*, and then I really panicked. This meant I must finish it. She got me an advance from Straight Arrow, which covered the return of the Prentice-Hall advance.

So I came to this desk in a window in Berkshire and I began again. It is now 1972, the early summer, and it is still not completed, and yet it is, because I am not going to write any more. I have done quite enough already. It is a book because it is a book.

I didn't have an English publisher, you know. I really wanted one, but couldn't see Macmillan liking it, or any of those serious people. Then a left-wing film-maker told Su Herbert who works for Davis-Poynter that I had written some lines and Su called me and said Mr Davis-Poynter (mister, yet) was interested and would like to see me. Then I am advised by Marxist subversives to take grimy Xeroxes, marked in blue by Alan Rinzler, American Publisher, with suggestions and corrections to Davis-Poynter.

Reg and me talk. I tell him it is OK stuff, you know . . . nice but naïve.

I leave Reg. Forget about it.

Reg rings me.

'I like it.'

'Then buy it.'

'I will.'

Reg becomes a new friend, introduces me to new friends. Isn't life great? Yes. Sometimes it really is.

Reg and I have not spoken for weeks. I have not spoken to Michael McIntyre who works with him either. I have been avoiding them. I have not returned their phone calls, I have not answered their notes. I have, however, had nightmares about them. I am filled with guilt. So this week I took time off to rewrite about ten thousand words. I have done that much. I also thought I might re-read Michael McIntyre's advice. Sample:

'As it now stands, the MS contains much amusing, informative, interesting material. The problem is that overall it lacks direction, depth and cohesion. One episode follows another – seemingly at random – with little attempt at interconnection and too often subjects are touched upon and swiftly left half explored. The result is that the total effect is rather bewildering. Most of all the MS lacks any sense of chronology and this makes it very difficult to discern any "theme" or development within it. And some sort of theme does seem very necessary to draw together the various episodes. Derek's philosophy would then fall naturally into place – rather than just appearing as it does now – uncomfortably sandwiched between things done/people met/places seen.'

I agree entirely.

Well, you know, I have written this book for the thousands and thousands and thousands of people who will enjoy it. I don't know whether it will have a really good sale but I don't care. It is very nice to make money but there are other things in life besides money. I am very happy that it is nearly over and by now it is a real honest pleasure writing to you out there from here.

THIS BOOK

I was born in Liverpool in 1932 and my parents raised me and my younger brother Bryan in nice little middle-class houses at the seaside in West Kirby, Cheshire – a lovely village where only man is vile. If you can live in West Kirby you can live anywhere.

My parents are clever. My father's trick lay in attracting people to him, adding younger and younger sets so that by the time he was old (and he is now eighty-two) he would still have friends young enough to be alive. My mother's genius was in organisation and in keeping things clean. They were good parents.

I went to a grammar school and I was bullied a lot but I was quick and unpredictable and I got by. I was very good at English and I worked for a local paper in West Kirby when I left school and I learned journalism and I loved it very much right up to 1964, when I left it to join Brian Epstein as his PA, working for the Beatles. I joined them because I wanted to work for them, that was all. I had been working for the *Daily Express* but you can only do that for so long without going mad.

I went mad anyway in 1964, and at the end of the year left the Beatles and went with Joan and our four children – Timothy, Gerard, Victoria and Vanessa – to Hollywood, movie capital of the world, where I became a publicist to dozens of very nice people in the music business. Joan and I grew up in California, found out a few things and took some of the dreaded LSD, and, finding we hadn't jumped out of any windows, we took some more. It felt fine.

In 1968 we came back to England and I rejoined the Beatles and Apple. This was when the book started and now, as I say, it is over. I work for Warner, Elektra and Atlantic Records now, in London, and I am extremely busy. So there, you see, it is not much of a story on the face of it, but behind the face all sorts of things are going on. We have six children now and life is pretty unsteady and very exciting. What else do you expect? It is late in the twentieth century.

I don't think that if you have a tidy mind you will find this book easy to follow. But who needs a tidy mind? Who has one? No one I know. Open it at any page. Keep it by the bed. It is written for you and only for you. You know who you are.

And I know who I am.

Derek Taylor, Sunningdale, Berkshire.

Yes sir, said the driver, yes siree, there ain't a funnier sight 'n all this world than a frightened coon. We were driving to the Indiana State Fair, him and me, and I had never been to Indiana before – nor since, thanks – so he was playing courier and guide. We had met a half-hour earlier in the courtyard at the motel on the outskirts of Indianapolis. The Beatles had been rushed into their limousine, a bad case of over-haste by panicky officials, and I had waved the car away as an alternative to losing an arm or maybe a life trying to climb in the front seat beside Brian Epstein who had been slammed in bodily. A local, a small, sandy, middle-American, came across to me and said: 'You missed your ride, buddy.' I said, yes, I had. 'I'll take you where you want to go,' he said. 'To the fair?'

I was grateful. We drove through a pretty neighbourhood, dressed in lovely green lawns and fine white houses and then we drove through another neighbourhood with brown lanes and fine black faces and he said: 'Coonsville. This is where "they" live; man these are some funny people. Catch one of them at night and put a scare in him and yes sir, there ain't a funnier sight in all the world than a frightened coon.'

He said how it was real funny that their eyes showed up round and white, y'know? Like Stepin Fetchit in the movies? Jesus, was this a man I was driving with; this was *my*

20

companion? He was the one man in the whole world I could trust to get me where I needed to be, and he was talking like this? Yes, oh yes, he was talking like this and I wasn't stopping him because I didn't know what to say to anyone like this because I didn't know till now that there *were* people like this, not who would come straight out with it. (Coons? I hadn't heard the word since the News Editor of the *Liverpool Daily Post* had let it drop once, many years ago, explaining that he was only using it affectionately. This was long before Johnny Speight's Garnett misfired and gave millions a racist vocabulary to be proud of.)

The driver said he had business in town and he was a family man and it was this way, like he had a son and it would make him a hero if he could get the boy to meet the Beatles, and it had come to him, like it was from heaven, that he had gotten to drive the Beatles' very own press agent to the State Fair'n all.

Oh yes? I not only had a bastard like this as a driver, but also I had got him for the rest of our stay in Indiana, which was another twenty-four hours. Again, Jesus!

Oh, you say, it is easy enough to shake the man off, kiss him good-bye with a 'go fuck yourself' at the gates to the fair, but when a man like that believes you owe him something (and I was now his passenger for free), you don't get rid so easily.

We arrived at the fair and he says he will bring the boy to the motel first thing tomorrow, or better still tonight, right? – and I will fix it for him to meet the four guys? Right?

The boy and the father came to the motel and they stayed and I had coffee with them and I had orange juice with them and I was very sorry for them and I hated them and I tried

to fix some sort of contact with the Beatles and I think I succeeded but I can't be sure because my memory fails me at this
point, and all I want to say is that if you are ever in Indiana
and you miss your ride, hire a cab because in the end it is not
as expensive as spending twenty-four hours of your precious
life with a bastard who throws scares into poor blacks just so
he can see the whites of their eyes, and who has a son whom
he is poisoning for the future.

I often think about this father and this son who so admired
the Beatles then and I wonder how they are shaping up to the
seventies. The boy will be at college now, I think. Is he freak
or straight? It would be fun to find out.

Many, if not most (and soon it will be all but a very few),
of the very early Beatles/Stones fans are married now, or
living like married, and from the evidence of record sales,
those bands have carried the support of most of them with
them into adulthood.

Are they not the protesters, the draft-resisters, the emancipated, the alienated and if they are not, how come they
heard the words of the songs and didn't heed them, for as
John Lennon said, 'Our songs were always about peace and
freedom and love, there was never any other message.' Is it
possible to march to war singing 'All You Need Is Love'? I
mean is it physically possible, emotionally possible?

The wife of the mayor of M in the USA came to visit us in
the summer of 1964. We were staying in the Something Hotel
in her husband's city and the Beatles were asleep after a
show the night before. It was the usual state of siege with the
street scene spilling into the hotel lobby and armed guards

everywhere. Pinkertons and cops and plainclothes men, men with short-sleeved white shirts and thin grey ties and short-sleeved white minds and thin grey thoughts, checking and re-checking passes and authorisations and the only person who reached us on our floor that morning was, naturally enough, the wife of the mayor. It was around eleven o'clock and I was asleep too. There was a knock at the door and a guy standing there said I had an important guest and I should be real nice to her on account of she was the wife of our mayor. Oh, great. I mean, really fantastic. I dressed and took two small yellow dexedrine tablets and cleaned my teeth and combed my hair and put on a tie – the essential routine of those days.

The wife of the mayor was in a room across the corridor and she had her daughter with her, a sweet little thing of nine, and there was also a reporter. The wife of the mayor said she had come to meet the Beatles and that was it. I said they were sleeping and she said that had nothing to do with her.

'Wake them.'

'Pardon me?'

'Get them up. I am not here to waste my time.'

I looked at the woman, I mean really looked at her. She was nice to look at, hard as hell but quite nice. I said I hadn't had breakfast but I was prepared to have a screwdriver if she would like to have a screwdriver. So we screwdrove together and she said she had been disgusted by the goings-on the night before, 'I mean, four young long-haired louts from nowhere messing up that fine auditorium and creating so much chaos and trouble that decent people trying to behave properly were prevented from going about their business.'

23

Oh?

'Nothing', she said, 'but nothing would have persuaded me to let my daughter into such an environment.' So what was her daughter doing right now, trying to meet the four louts?

'I am insisting upon it because these four people are in our city and in their way they are famous,' and, she said, they had a fascination for her daughter which, though incomprehensible, was something that had to be faced in the proper time and in the proper place. The point was, she said, that right now was the time and right here, in the Something Hotel, was the place. But the Beatles are sleeping, I said, and she said she heard me before, but I didn't appear to have heard her.

'Get them up. They have no business to be asleep at this time of day.'

And, she said – and don't take me lightly, she said – there was this reporter who would bear witness to my refusal, my outright refusal, to let the daughter of the Mayor of M meet these four boys who had received so much money for a half-hour show which no one could hear. The reporter, a plain and pleasant girl of about twenty, blushed. It was getting very heavy. The wife of the Mayor of M said, further, that while she had the opportunity to talk to a visiting Englishman, she would like to make it clear that M was a very fine place to live, and it was in no way to be confused with Chicago which was a dirty, corrupt and badly administered city.

Phew.

Wow.

Oh, well . . . there is no punchline to this; the daughter of the Mayor of M got to meet the Beatles later that day. Did you doubt she would?

24

3 / Of 1970 and the years before – written 1969–70. Some who died and some who lived

Sharon Tate was murdered yesterday in a house in Bel Air where Joan and I went to a party one night long ago and admired the mock oak beams on which the killers would hang the dead, eight-month-pregnant body of Sharon Tate, and admired, too, the grounds where they would stretch out three others described by the papers as 'fully dressed in hippy type garb'. Pretty nasty.

Terry Melcher and Mark Lindsay lived in the place before Sharon Tate. The house she and her friends died in was protected by an electrical gate. Joan and I didn't understand it when we arrived for Terry Melcher's party, we didn't know what it was. We'd never spoken to anyone from a gate and had it opened by remote control. Boy, were we naive! Steve Sanders was there that night. Steve wasn't naive. He had gatecrashed better parties than this one and he climbed the gate and got himself in a fine state of indignation when he was asked to leave.

Steve brings good things to the Big Stars and sometimes they thank him and sometimes they share it with him, but not always, not always. Stars become so used to those who bring them things that they sort of take them for granted.

Steve is known as the Bomber sometimes, because he

'bombs' – he fails to deliver, he just doesn't make it across the line in time. Not always, but sometimes and you only have to bomb sometimes in Hollywood to be known as the Bomber. If Brian Wilson, Giant Beach Boy, can become a genius on the basis of what he achieved, then Steve Sanders can sure as hell become a genius on the basis of what he doesn't get together.

Once he was Mamas and Papas' road manager; Lou Adler, who produced them, told me he failed to get the Mamas and Papas to an aircraft on time. They all missed it but Steve put matters right by hiring a Lear jet. He climbed aboard and the pilot took off and reached 42,000 feet in fifteen minutes and Steve was well pleased and very relieved but he had forgotten that the Mamas and Papas were still grounded. He smiled to himself, no doubt because he is a happy soul, easily pleased, and me and a thousand others really like him.

Steve was a pal of John's once, John Lennon; I think he still is; John liked his impudence and charm and optimism and hedonism. Steve is a man who didn't really give a shit, as long as he was near to the great, or near to the near-greats who could lead him to the greats, so that he could give them good things to make them happy. John gave Steve a few movie cameras and a crate of film and bankrolled Steve from Weybridge which is in Surrey, England to Monterey which is in California, USA, to shoot a movie on the Monterey pop festival. He arrived, 700 miles later, and was thrown out of the concert area so many times – because film rights had been sold to ABC for half a million bucks.

Steve didn't get to shoot the concerts but somehow he made a movie on the pop festival and he enjoys seeing it and showing it and even Stars enjoy it. If you consider the following facts – that the Monterey Pop Festival was the first great festival in the brief and furious history of pop music, and that Steve Sanders not only got in for nothing, but, for free and against terrific odds, made a movie of it as well, and came as the representative of John Lennon of the Famous Beatles, then maybe Bomber is not the right way to describe Steve Sanders.

The pop fringe is a strange piece of fabric, it is woven by many hands, not all of them skilled, but to the last tattered strand, it involves only the dedicated, and many of the people without a specific role have a far warmer sensitivity to the pulse of the lifestyle of the artists than the men who claim a knowing and important role – the bookers, the entrepreneurs, the agents, the impresarios, the press.

There is a man called Alan Pariser who has a chalet with a view of Hollywood you wouldn't believe, and if you are anyone in pop you know Alan Pariser and he knows you. He, too, has sweets for the sweet and sugar for his honey. He married the daughter of the Duke of Newcastle. He is bearded and mostly wears shades and a cowboy hat and drives a Porsche.

Alan was born into a rich Midwest family who made paper cups in Michigan. He is still well off, it would seem, and he will lend money to anyone he likes. He is a good kind man who knows so much that I reckon if my morbid curiosity cannot be assuaged by tonight's BBC TV news on the Tate murders (and it is a light appetite which is satisfied by a BBC TV news bulletin), I can call Alan in Hollywood and if he is not able to offer any new *facts* on the Sharon Tate 'ritual slaying', then he would be ready and able to offer views and opinions substantial enough to meet any whim or quirk, however fanciful.

It was Alan Pariser who thought of having a pop festival,

and came to me and also to Ben Shapiro (of whom, a little more later) – and so was launched the Monterey International Pop Festival which was going to make a lot of money until John Phillips of the Mamas and Papas and Lou Adler came to lead the festival and took it off Pariser and Shapiro and made it non-profitmaking and made Pariser nonproducer and whipping boy.

Alan knows the Beatles, he is George's Los Angeles guide, stays in Palm Springs when he pleases, has toured with Cream, launched Delaney and Bonnie, helped to make *You Are What You Eat,* a movie of mixed virtues and vices, looks forward to being around when the next Thing happens, and undoubtedly will be. If I am around, I will always want Pariser to be alive somewhere, making his transatlantic telephone calls, hustling deals which will make loads of waves and hardly any money.

Ben Shapiro made a movie with Woody Allen and has had other adventures in many areas, is a friend of Miles Davis, finds the truth stranger than fiction and has plumped for fiction – was an early admirer and booker of Lenny Bruce and is now well woven into the fringe. Ben was emptied out of the Monterey Festival by Adler and Phillips – probably wisely, for neither unit sat comfortably with the other – and after making a statement in the trade papers that he left 'amicably to press on with many movie commitments' – a statement so full of lies that it made me, who drafted it, reach for another capsule-ful of courage (my second by lunchtime) – was given $5,000, and, as far as I know, bears no grudges and lives in Mexico.

It was a sad affair, the Shapiro story, cruel in its way and out of place in the music industry which, though it may be written of as 'cruel' and 'a jungle' by journalists far beyond the fringe, is not really cruel at all – as businesses go – but rather an amiable and friendly milieu, at least that is how I find it. As friendly, anyway, as the press. Ah, the press . . . the Gentlemen of the Press. A gentleman of the press once was I, believing it to be my life's work and a Duty. Alas, poor Derek, I knew him well in his blue raincoat smelling horribly of beer and doing his best for his paper and for himself and for his contacts and so compromising all along the line that it is a wonder he can still look his clippings full in the fading type-face. No longer a watchdog, and lacking the curiosity and fear of failure which prompted him once to kick doors down, he would be a useless man to any newsdesk nowadays.

Your newspaper reporter lives in a strange and frightening world, oversimplified by the need to write in baby-talk, over-complicated because the reporter is never told the whole truth.

It is a world where human torches run down streets of fear in villages of wagging tongues, where police battle, where tracker dogs hunt, where judges lash rapists and govern-ments are flayed by the opposition, where tug-of-love babies wrench heartstrings, where men fall hundreds of feet and live/die, where mayhem, murder, fire and drowning haunt families of eight, where teenage couples elope and stars con-fess they have been fools and spent all on the champagne life, where chess players wreak havoc and unions hold the coun-try to ransom, where women weep and children play happily among swirling, poisonous fumes.

For a week or two it is OK, even exciting. After fifteen years, which is how long I lived in it, it becomes a pain.

4 / About 1965–68 – written 1970.
Leonard

Leonard Grant had an office next to mine on the eighth floor of the 9000 building on Sunset Boulevard in Hollywood. He managed Frank Gorshin (*Batman*'s TV 'Riddler') and also Captain Beefheart and his Magic Band whom he wanted 'cleaning up and selling to the fans'. Captain Beefheart came from the High Desert, from Lancaster and he wanted to sing blues, just sing blues man.

I wanted to 'sell him to the fans' as we would say then, because I needed the money and it was true that for those days, the Captain was very eccentric. This was 1966, a very hard year. I was taking on too much. Leonard Grant said Beefheart was not made of money so would I keep the price modest because Beefheart would be the one who was paying. We agreed, asked $250 a month, and most months I got it. The first thing to do was hear Beefheart sing. I liked him very much; he was a very funny man, wry and dry and he sang a very hard mean blues, cupping his hand over his right ear. He complained all the time that the sound system was shit, just shit man. This was at a club on Santa Monica Boulevard. (I forget the name. It may come back to me later; we shall see.) 'I'll take them,' I said generously. Would they take me?

Leonard Grant told them I was very impressive and witty, a hard role to play all the time. I was so impressive and witty that when I wrote one of the most impressive and witty and far-out 'biographies' I had ever done, by night, on dexedrines too many to count between the whiskies, Leonard Grant took hold of a corner of it and waved it as if to shake the germs away and said, This is not at all what I wanted. You're making fun of my group.'

I should have known then we wouldn't make it together, Leonard Grant and I. To tell you how far the relationship deteriorated I should say that the last time we corresponded it was over who should pay for the damage done to a mimeograph machine which he had stored in my office because it was too old and ugly for his but not, he assumed, for mine.

A piece of hard plastic cowling had been damaged on the machine – I had smashed it one morning after too many brandies for breakfast. Instead of hitting Leonard Grant, I had punched the shit out of the plastic, bashed it, crashing my fist up and down until the skin broke and blood was drawn. 'I think it must have fallen,' I told Leonard Grant. Fallen? He didn't believe me and sued for damages.

But that lay in the future. The issue in the beginning was how to get Captain Beefheart's ugly mug in *16 Magazine*, preferably on the cover along with Mark Lindsay and Jim McGuinn. Well, for a start, that *hair*, Captain? And those clothes? He had hair down to his shoulders and jeans, and if you think that isn't far out, well you're right but how long is your memory? Nobody with hair down to his shoulders and jeans made the charts, not even the Byrds were that outrageous in 1966. I remember Gene Clark of the Byrds coming back to LA after a trip to San Francisco and saying, 'I like long hair but those cats in San Francisco! It's going too far!'

31

Leonard Grant had a nice woman working for him in those days. Together the nice lady and I took the Captain and the Magic Band to De Voss and other boutiques on Hollywood Boulevard and dressed them in big-collared shirts and ties and jackets and boots and we had their hair cut. Their hair cut? Oh yes. One afternoon I hired a barber to cut their hair. So silly.

At first Captain Beefheart didn't make a lot of space while we worked together, but we did work hard and we amused each other very much; and later both he and I left Leonard Grant who had really strayed out of his market in the first place. It was the middle period of the new rock'n'roll and the smooth old world was becoming involved with the newer elements. Foolishly. The men in suits needed to find out what was happening. A lot of them drowned in the process. Well, anyway, the nearest Captain Beefheart and I got to a spread was in *Flip* magazine, published with some skill and energy by one Stephen Kahn of the Kahn Communications Corporation of New York City. Kahn and I had a deal whereby I would wreck my health writing about my clients and he would print what I wrote, but only if the groups were making it anyway. As a concession to the unknown Beefheart, he agreed to reproduce a collage made for me by one of the Magic Band. It looked very good but it had no more to do with The Blues than Rex Harrison has to do with Sly Stone.

All this for $250 a month? Yes. It was really a rugged fight for us publicists then. We didn't know our rights and we didn't smoke dope and we, well we just had to learn that the only thing that mattered was the music, the music, and that when Beefheart said all he wanted to do was sing blues, he should have been allowed to sing blues. Fame was the spur that blinded us.

Now, right now, Beefheart is on the cover of as many rock magazines and newspapers as he cares to be. It is just amazing. He wears whatever he pleases and his hair is like yours and mine and he still sings the blues and he hasn't had a hit or played Carnegie Hall or Shea Stadium or anything; but what the hell! He is Captain Beefheart and he should worry.

He called me once, at five in the morning or some time like that. 'Hey man, will Apple sign me up? I can't stand these people who own us. Their heads are so small man, forget it.' Apple didn't sign him up and he is better off where he is. He is with WEA Records and so am I. Saw him yesterday. Nice.

Captain Beefheart and the Byrds, and also Tiny Tim, were good enough to perform free at a benefit concert I had promoted for myself in March 1968 on the eve of de-immigrating from California back to Liverpool. I had made quite a lot of money one way or another during our three years in Hollywood, but I didn't seem to have much left when it came to booking an air ticket home to Liverpool, so, at the last moment, I invited about 500 people to come to Ciro's on the Strip for a farewell party. Cost per ticket: $5.50. People responded very well – such is Hollywood, there is a lot of goodwill among the panic – and 600 came, but I over-ordered on the wine (most of the guests were wiped out by cannabis) and underestimated the gatecrashing. There was quite a deficit. About $2,000.

It was an excellent party and Beefheart complained like hell about the sound system so, I guess, it was a success.

33

The party at Ciro's was a fine bold stroke, but then it was Hollywood, Hollywood, and it didn't strike me till later, as I wondered how any of it had happened, wondering if any of it *had* happened. So much living was crammed into the three years we spent in Hollywood. We flew out of Liverpool in 1965 and sailed back into Liverpool in 1968 totally changed, totally. We didn't feel 'British' any more and a good thing too. We belonged, we believed, to a brotherhood in rock'n'roll which had nothing to do with where we were born but which had everything to do with 'where our heads were at, man', as the saying went.

We had learned so much from the young and from the music in America. From Beefheart, from the Byrds, from the Beach Boys, from the Southern Californian experience which is like no other. I cannot describe the Californian experience which is like no other. You just have to go there and do it and rely on your ability to absorb it and still stay alive and reasonably steady. If you can do it there, you can do it anywhere. Do what? Do anything. The Beach Boys, born there, successful there, crazy there, completely re-born there, they are as good an example of what Southern California is – erratic, self-indulgent, optimistic, large, vain, and full of innovation.

Often put down in their early years, now vastly and widely appreciated in so many, many ways, the Beach Boys and I met in 1966 and we worked together for two years. They paid me $750 a month for publicity and all sorts of help and they loaned me five thou, when I had a crisis. Such generosity, but Christ, they were hard work. The basis of the band was the three Wilson brothers, Brian, Dennis and Carl, and their cousin Mike Love, but there was a fifth, Al Jardine, at that time, not a full-sharing financial partner, and there was a sixth, Bruce Johnston, stand-in for Brian during stage performances, not yet certain of his role (he has since left; he left in 1972) and they were anxious to bring everything much more together and win a wider following among the *cognoscenti*. They were on the threshold of releasing *Pet Sounds* and the next single was to be 'Good Vibrations'. I wrote many words on them over the years. It reads kinda corny now, but it was OK for its time:

I'm sure I don't need to tell you how great the Beach Boys are – you will all have had ample evidence, visually and musically, of the creative, vital, outgoing energies of this all-American fivesome, who comprise the most powerful pop unit in the USA.

What I would like to do is to elaborate on the special qualities which have taken the Beach Boys to the pinnacle of home-grown entertainment in little more than four and a half years.

I believe their chief assets are the close intelligent relationship between the members of the group bound together by the genius of Brian, the eldest of the three Californian Wilson brothers and – though you don't see him on stage any more – still undisputed group leader.

Brian, Carl and Dennis Wilson, their cousin, Mike Love, and their long-time friends, Al Jardine and Bruce Johnston, are now solidly ahead of every competitor in what is becoming a very hard-fought pop battle.

None of the talented newcomers who crashed into the charts in the coast-to-coast music explosion last year would pretend that they are in a position to assail the Beach Boys' hard-won status.

In record sales (fifteen million singles; eight million-dollar albums, and five others nearing that figure) they may never be overtaken.

As a personal appearance attraction they draw bigger audiences than any other group in the world – with the exception of the Beatles, who do not, in any case, tour America as extensively as the Beach Boys.

For musical expansion and development, no group or individual in the US has made so much progress in so short a time as Brian Wilson and his friends.

So what is it that keeps them so completely ahead, so totally in control and so comfortably unchallengeable?

Maybe Brian Wilson can illuminate this by stating his aims. For his aims are so clear and his priority so exact that the outcome must be good.

'The thing is I write and think in terms of what the Beach Boys can do. Not what they would find it easy to do, but what I know they are capable of doing, which isn't always the same thing.

'I have a governor in my mind, which keeps my imagination in order because idiot ideas are just a hand-out. But I don't like to be told it can't be done when I know it can. That's the point. It mostly can be done.

'My musical influences go back to the early days when I worshipped the Four Freshmen, those great guys. That groovy sectional sound!

'The Beach Boys are so lucky . . . we have a high range of voices; Mike can go from bass to the E above middle C; Dennis, Carl and Al progress upwards through C, A and D. I can take the second D in the second clef.

'The harmonies we were able to produce is a uniqueness which is really the only important thing you can put into

36

records – some quality no one else has got into.'

Brian adds: 'I love peaks in a song – and enchanting them on the control panel. Most of all, I love the human voice for its own sake. But I can treat it with some detachment, as another musical instrument. This doesn't imply a lack of respect, because I respect all instruments – from Jews' harps to spinets.

'I know that in some circles, we're not regarded as all that "hip" or "in". This is maybe because we haven't just arrived from nowhere with something new with a new label.

'But I don't care too much what anyone says, so long as I know I'm staying ahead – right up to the limit of my present capabilities. I don't put out anything I don't respect. And I know for sure that the Beach Boys' fans agree that the group most certainly brought something new into rock'n'roll.'

They brought in their incomparable harmonies, their healthy, youthful feeling for the spirit of California, their uncompromising adherence to their own sound – uncompromising not because they won't admit new influences on their music, but because however much they draw from the contemporary scene, they remain, bell clear, THE BEACH BOYS.

No one has ever said: 'Who's that?' when a new Beach Boys record is launched on the air.

Every good artist wants recognition from fellow-artists. Bogart dug Lionel Barrymore; and *vice versa*. Joan Crawford admires Bette Davis. So OK. The Beach Boys have won the adulation of the Beatles, and it works the other way as well. Ask any one of either group.

But the Beach Boys were particularly concerned that their new album *Pet Sounds* should indicate to the Beatles (and the Stones whom they also admire) that America, through the

Beach Boys, was as far ahead in musical trends as Britain.

And sure enough, the acknowledgement came instantly and without prompting. Beatle George Harrison and Stones' manager, Andrew Oldham, had the first copies of *Pet Sounds* in Britain. George was swift to the telephone to spend an hour in over-flowing admiration, and Oldham spent an entire night sitting by his phonograph with the album on 'repeat'. In the morning (California time), he stammered out a string of adjectives of overwhelming praise.

Let's go back to the beginning of this extraordinary success story. Let's go to Hawthorne, on the edge of the Pacific, where the Wilson brothers, Mike Love and Al Jardine went to school.

It was 1961 and pop music throughout the world was limp and lame and meandering. There was no known direction for the tired stragglers from the rock'n'roll race of the 1950s and none of the Beach Boys would pretend that when they went into a little studio to record a song called 'Surfin'' they intended to change the entire course of contemporary music.

Yet, on the suggestion of sixteen-year-old Dennis Wilson, Mike Love and Brian wrote 'Surfin'' to reflect the sounds and essence of a musical adventure which is still – though wildly exciting and successful – only in its early stages.

'Surfin'' was recorded in two hours in Hollywood, on a single-track tape system, with Al Jardine playing standard double-bass twice as big as himself, fourteen-year-old Carl Wilson on acoustic guitar, Brian himself standing up using brushes on drums, and Mike Love singing the vocals with a severe cold.

The record sold more than 40,000 copies in the dying weeks of 1961. And it went to Number 3 in Southern California in a chart distorted beyond belief by the Twist and its many variants. (Chubby Checker was Number 1 at the time.)

In the US as a whole, the record reached 75. From this first single, the Beach Boys drew about $300 in royalties – sufficient to take them back into the studio for another single, 'Surfin' Safari'. This, coupled with '409', was released by Capitol.

It was a big nationwide hit, and the Boys started to perform locally; then nationally; and by 1963 were a prosperous, virile, national touring group and massive hitmakers, in a period when, otherwise, American pop music was still in a dead faint.

There is a very close family-feeling within the group. There are, of course, the three Wilson brothers: Brian, Dennis, Carl, cousin Mike Love and friend-near-enough-relative Al Jardine. Plus 'phantom' Beach Boy Bruce Johnston, for personal appearances. He has known the other Beach Boys long enough to be in on the tight family unit.

Says Brian: 'The secret of our success is that we have writer, arranger, producer and artists, all in one package. The more self-contained you are in this work, the tighter you can be, and the longer you can last.'

His own Beverly Hills home has a completely equipped sound studio, where he can experiment with new sounds, embellish the old ones and work out more hits for the group.

Their TV appearances on the Jack Benny, Andy Williams and Ed Sullivan shows have proved that they are as big on the small screen as they are on the concert platform.

When asked if they still worry about their next single becoming a hit, Mrs Wilson (the mother of three BBs) said: 'Brian goes through panicsville every time a new record is released.' Carl says: 'For about two weeks after a song is out, Brian will say, "This one's a bomb . . . I just know it" and worries like crazy. Then when he sees it enter the charts he stops worrying – until the next one comes out.'

Carl described what he felt was the Beach Boys' basic appeal: 'I think we represent young California in both our music and our physical image. While it isn't essential here in California, it makes a tremendous impact in the Eastern States and in foreign countries.'

Their dominance on the international scene has taken them, so far, to Britain, France, Italy, Sweden, New Zealand, Australia, Denmark, Holland, Germany, Canada and the Far East, including, of course, Japan where they had a quite sensational two-week concert tour.

The Beach Boys became very fashionable in Europe at the time I was with them. I don't know why. They'd been around for years, making an absolute fortune and spending it. In Britain they once unseated the fab Beatles from Fave Group, but such polls are without much merit, I think. Richard Goldstein, small, earnest, *Village Voice, New York Times* – he who hated *Sgt Pepper* – came to see me once and said all the really hip people were thinking of having their own polls to show who the top people actually were. He said that if *we* were to be polled then an *important* conclusion could be reached.

I doubt it. Leave it to the public – to you and me; look at our own private record collections, watch which concerts we *pay* to see. That is the only test.

Pop writers were making names for themselves by 1966–7. I took Tom Nolan to meet Brian Wilson one afternoon. Tom was very young then and terribly bright and cool. He had awful acne and he wasn't handsome but his prose was good. Brian found him a fine listener and that suited Brian very well because he was a fine talker. When he tried, he could give fantastic interviews. When he tried he could make fantastic records. Long live the Beach Boys and may Brian Wilson rejoin them.

About Tom Nolan; he wrote in the *LA Times* Brian had taken *acid* and nobody, but nobody, got upset. I suppose you have to call it *LSD* before the bogeyman can assume a shape worthy of fear and hate. When Paul McCartney was asked whether he had taken LSD, he said, 'Yes' and after *Life* had printed it, TV interviewers asked him didn't he think it was irresponsible for a man in his public position (oh *really?*) to influence others to take LSD? Paul asked the TV interviewers didn't they know it would be irresponsible of them to broadcast that he had taken LSD? Oh, wait a moment . . . Well, the television interviewers *did* broadcast it, so what with their irresponsibility and Paul's, I guess some people did follow his example. OK.

Pete Johnson is another writer who let his hair hang out. I met him at a Beefheart gig in the Whisky à Go Go. Leonard Grant and I had rowed for much of the afternoon over which disc jockeys would sit where (such trivia, it makes me wonder sometimes), and it was quite a disappointing evening, presswise, in that not too many pressmen came. In fact, only red-haired Pete Johnson came and he was late and missed Beefheart's first set. The Doors were on, with the Captain, as second act. Hardly anyone had heard of them, hardly anyone except all the people who had always known how good they were which didn't include me, not until that night.

Pete came in raving about the Doors and complaining about the aggravation he had to take from doorkeepers. I bought him a whisky and then I bought Joan and me cognac and Pete started raving again about the amazing Doors. I hoped that he would like the Captain too and he did. He wrote something nice in the *Los Angeles Times* and Pete Johnson became a well-known critic in Los Angeles. Then a wicked man laid a joint on him, then another, and before you could say Pete Johnson, Pete Johnson had red hair down to his elbows and no desire to be a critic of *any*-thing, let alone something as nice as music. He too works for WEA.

I worked for the Doors much later, when they were about to peak. Their management, called A. Associate and Associates or some such thing, called me in and said they had heard good things about me and I said I had heard good things about them which was a downright lie because I had heard nothing about them at all, but I loved the Doors.

The deal lasted a week, during which I arranged one interview and then I wandered through Beverly Hills with them talking about colour transparencies. I couldn't make it with the management nor they with me. Managements can be very strange. The Doors left them too; it always happens. I wrote to the management and said: 'Can't make it man, dunno why,' and they wrote back 'OK, here's $500, your fee.' (Shows there's good and bad in all of us. Five hundred dollars for a week!)

Charlie Green and Brian Stone, brilliant delinquent brains behind Sonny and Cher and other Great Adventures of the sixties, hired me to do the Buffalo Springfield, another group I liked front and backstage, and Charlie gave me $100 in green in advance. Very nice, I thought, and spent it that day, or maybe a week earlier and a coupla months later I wrote to Charlie and Brian saying; 'Let's call the whole thing off.' Time dims my motives and I can only suppose I couldn't take the added responsibility. Hollywood was getting very weird by then and it was only a matter of time, I thought, before I represented every group in town and went absolutely crazy. I realised something was going wrong when I was picking up famous bands and dropping them a week later.

I hadn't paid any tax in two years and I'd saved nothing so that when the taxman came to see me on the eighth floor of the 9000 building, I was in no position to pay him. I told him so, frankly, and he betrayed less interest than if I'd been Brigitte Bardot, nude in his kitchen sink, though not much less. He questioned me for about six hours and in the end, I thanked him for his enormous courtesy and offered him an album by Chad and Jeremy whom I also represented. He refused to be swayed into showing any humanity and said that it could be construed as a bribe which, he explained, he was not empowered to accept, and also 'I do not have a record player, at this time. Sir.

'I shall return tomorrow,' he said, and he did, having given me twenty-four hours to find two and a half g's which I did in the nick of time by scoring the five I told you about, from the Beach Boys.

Times were tough, reader. I fired everyone, particularly my clients who were all driving me out of my mind. They all forgave me and they left graciously and almost all of them paid me, some twice over, even Paul Revere, a parsimonious and honest man, of whom, as follows . . .

5 / About 1965–68 – written 1970.
New chapter

Paul Revere and the Raiders were the first group I signed when I emigrated to America with Joan and the four oldest children in 1965. The group were handed to me by a man named Bob Eubanks who fronts the awful *Newly-Weds* gameshow on American television. Have you seen the *Newly-Weds*? It is David and Julie, on toast. The aim is to find how much the newly-weds really know about each other, e.g. What would your husband say if he farted: (a) I regret farting (b) I don't regret farting (c) I guess I farted, or (d) who farted?

Bob Eubanks is the ideal man for this show. He ran clean clubs for teens; these newly-weds were *his* kids, grown to . . . maturity? When he hired me he was the man who promoted the Beatles in LA. I was never really sure he liked them, but the hell, he was getting rich at the Hollywood Bowl. There were many other deals going. One of the drivers, after the first Bowl show, handed the Beatles towels to dry their sweat. He later cut up the towels, encased half-inch squares of towel in plastic, and sold them for five bucks each. The driver was really a radio station newsman. I guess he's got turned on by now, but in those days he wasn't very cool. It was all deals then.

Anyway, I got to know Eubanks during our first American visit, with the Beatles in 1964, and he said whydoncher work for me buddy, we'll get rich?

So our family of six emigrated. Eubanks gave me $215 a week and an office at 6290 Sunset Boulevard and we called it Prestige Publicity. Prestige? I had a high-backed leather chair and a couple of partners called Gayle and Cecil Tuck, from Texas, hoping to make it big in rock'n'roll. They were all very good to Joan and me in their way, but they were in one hell of a hurry to make it. They made us welcome and then put me to work like a kilo of grass, spreading me around like a mass turn-on. I was the guy who had publicised the Beatles and I could make anyone famous. If you rolled me up and smoked me, you would be on *The Ed Sullivan Show* come Independence Day. Bob Eubanks took me up and down the Boulevard to get me noticed, like Tom Ewell did to Jayne Mansfield in *The Girl Can't Help It.*

It was really tortuous because so many lies had been told that before anyone could talk terms (importuners or importuned) there had to be a general suspension of disbelief.

Me, I believed everything. Bob took me to see the father of Dick Dale (and the Del-Tones), a man called James Monsour, who told me Elvis was a fraud. The real king was Dick Dale. I went out to Harmony Park ballroom at Anaheim, where Dick Dale held dances weekly, and it was clear he was making a fortune. But, by then, we'd seen the Byrds and compared to them, Dick Dale, man? Forget it. Bob took me to meet Lloyd Thaxton then running dance shows on TV. Lloyd I liked, and he me, but short of having me sit on a throne answering questions about the Beatles on camera, he couldn't fit me into his format.

I was taken to meet Alan Bernard, Andy Williams's manager. He also had Roger Miller in those days. Alan is definitive

Hollywood, very well fed and very smooth, rich and full of experience. Bob wanted to sign Roger Miller for publicity, Roger Miller had just had four pages or more in *Life* magazine, but Bob reckoned we could do a better job. I wished he could have told me how, because when Alan Bernard asked me how, I said, 'I don't know', which was not a very satisfactory answer.

Another place we went was Crescendo Records, then managed by Bud Dain who later married Jackie DeShannon, and also a big man with United Artists. Bud told me he liked my shirt and I said I would try and get him one. (I did try, and tried very hard, not realising that it had just been warm Hollywood social talk from Bud. He couldn't care less whether or not he had a shirt like mine. How much did *I* have to learn?) Bud gave me the singers Joe and Eddie and it was nice meeting Bud, but it wasn't lining Eubank's pocket, me signing Joe and Eddie.

Before we went to live in America, when I was with the Beatles and I was being softened up before emigrating, I was taken to San Francisco to meet the Beau Brummels. Dinner was bought for all of us, and for a couple of the Beau Brummels, on Brian Epstein's tab in the Hilton Hotel. I later signed the Beau Brummels and made the mistake of taking them to see the Byrds, whom I also represented and who were then just beginning. The Brummels's manager, Carl Scott murmured: 'This smells like competition' (remember that at the turn of 1964–5, the two groups poised to become America's answer to the Beatles and Gerry and the Pacemakers – oh yes – were the Beau Brummels and Paul Revere and the Raiders) and he fired me for divided loyalties. Carl Scott now manages Captain Beefheart and Sal Valentino of the Brummels went on to form another band – 'Stoneground'. Small world.

So, as we were saying a page or so back, I began my career as puppet head of Prestige Publicity with Paul Revere and the Raiders and the Beau Brummels, plus a watching brief (and no income) for Joe and Eddie and 5 per cent of a singer called Jerry Naylor who was once with the Crickets. My friend, Curt Gunther, a melancholy photographer in his forties, with credits all over the media and no faith in mankind, took me aside my first night in 6290 Sunset Boulevard and, drawing back a curtain, pointed to a flashing sign in Vine Street: SEABOARD LOANS. 'That's where a scene like this ends,' he said with pessimism. Three years later, after all my furniture had been packed ready to return to England and Apple, I looked through the bills outstanding and, indeed, we did owe a few hundred to Seaboard Loans, for a colour television set. Paid it all since, plus hundreds and hundreds of dollars interest.

Paul Revere and the Raiders, the Beau Brummels, Joe and Eddie and Jerry Naylor. Plus the Beatles, for though I wasn't working for them any more they were the love of my life and Bob Eubanks figured that with a love like that you know it can't be bad.

'I'm going to have you fly to the Bahamas,' he said, the night we arrived in Los Angeles, 70,000 miles from England and intending to set up home.

'Tonight?'

'No. Next week.'

Gee, thanks. Maybe we can get a house, find schools, buy some furniture, get used to the heat and, all in one week, fly to the Bahamas.

And, also, he said, why didn't I fly to Sacramento, see Paul Revere and the Raiders, make friends, sign them up and go on stage to say: 'Hi. I'm Derek Taylor, used to work for the Beatles. I'm now working for Paul Revere and I'm flying to the Bahamas next week to see the Beatles make their new movie and I'm going to take them your love and also the good wishes of Paul Revere and the Raiders.' I guessed this must be how things work in America, so I did it. I made friends with Paul Revere, signed them up and went on stage and made my speech. Later that night, I went to the motel where Revere and company were staying and he showed me how you could put a match to a fart and there would be green flame. I quite liked the guy. I liked the group too. They were good and they did well.

They were all young then (all but Revere and Mark Lindsay who had seen a lot of hard service here and there), and full of hope of taking over from the Beatles. 'Are we good enough?' they asked and it was tough to answer 'No', so one just hedged and mumbled and begged the question.

The next week I flew to the Bahamas with Dave Hull, squarest disc jockey at KRLA, an amiable short-hair who believed that Medicare had to be the worst thing to happen to America since the New Deal.

We arrived in Nassau to find the Beatles just leaving for dinner in the town. They were less than glad to see me, old pal in radio drag with a tape-recorder over my shoulders.

'This is Derek Taylor, reporting from the Bahamas. I have

49

with me Ringo Starr of the Beatles. Hi Ringo. Nice to see you again.'

'Hi Derek. Nice to see you again. What are *you* doing with a microphone under my famed nose?'

What indeed?

Bob's idea was that I would use my relationship with them, my friendship even, and get interviews which would be unique: 'Not merely interviews, but rather . . . conversation between friends' was the slogan we would use to sell the tapes, once they had been cut up, packaged and prepared for use on radio stations. A scale of charges was drawn up – $50, $100, $200, depending on the wattage of the station.

None of this was to be communicated to the Beatles. All they were to know was that Derek was doing a little gig for KRLA to get Prestige Publicity some working capital.

Before the family and I had arrived in Los Angeles, there had been dozens of commercials on KRLA: 'Derek Taylor is jetting to town. Derek Taylor? Wow. Yes, folks, Derek Taylor is coming to KRLA.'

Also, above my glamorous name, letters had gone to every showbiz celebrity in town, announcing my coming. Oh, yes, it's all true.

Paul was very mean in the Bahamas. I mean, mean. Who is to blame him? Not I. Not me. 'Bloody hell,' he said when he saw me. 'Bloody hell, Derek. You with a tape-recorder asking us questions?' Oh yes, me with a tape-recorder. The thing was what was the thing I was? Their friend or a journalist or their ex-publicist Brian Epstein's ex-personal assistant or a puppet of Bob Eubanks or a man in search of a career in

American radio or what? The answer is I didn't think there was any choice. I didn't know about things like that. I mean I wouldn't rob an old woman with one leg and a blind dog, and I wouldn't take a bribe and I wouldn't rape my sister but I would do many, many things if I was told to because that was the way it had always been. I would write a list of Forty Fab Facts you didn't know about the Beatles and sell them. I would allow myself to be offered to Lloyd Thaxton of Hollywood as a television link-man, I would do so many things which now would be quite ridiculous. I would, even, have the extraordinary cheek to turn up in the Bahamas with a tape-recorder to interview the Beatles. It was as well I did it then; I couldn't do it now. God, I must have been brave or daft or something I'm not sure any more.

Brian had slipped out of the Bahamas before I arrived. A good idea. We hadn't been very close since the previous year, 1964, when I had resigned in the Riviera Motel near Kennedy Airport. It was a shame because we lost valuable talking-time and he hadn't very long to live and many, many people with whom Brian had trouble have their own regrets that their patience was not more extensive and, of course, patience was what you needed with Brian because he could be, if not impossible, then unbearable, and sometimes impossibly unbearable, but many of the people I like most are absolutely terrible. You too? Good.

We were down on the beach at Paradise Island (you reached it by ferry from Nassau; in those days it was owned by Huntington Hartford, later Howard Hughes) and it was a fantastic rich man's folly with a casing like a palace out of

Ben Hur, quite empty, safe doors swinging open, phones out of order – open to wind and water. The beaches that *were* Paradise, empty but for Beatles paying gold for the privilege, and an army of savage extras, one of whom was Murray the K, disc jockey lately become fifth Beatle and anxious to appear in a movie with them. ('For the image, man.') Down on the beach at Paradise Island, Dave Hull had one recorder and mike, I had another. He had given me his mike: 'This will put more oomph' (oomph, for Chrissake?) 'in your voice,' he said, showing me. 'Moooore ba-aaaaasssss sound, like, deeeeeep.' OK Dave, I can dig it. The mike was faulty and I popped p's in the breeze.

We split up between the Beatles. I took John first; caustic John who was really nothing of the sort. He pulled a couple of desultory put-downs and then gave me as good a tape as you'll get if you are asking questions like: 'Whereja buy your boots?' and 'Do you enjoy filming?' and 'How old are you?' of someone you know at least as well as your brother, and maybe better.

George told me about going to a family wedding in Liverpool. Paul decided not to be mean any longer – guessing, correctly, that life was bad enough without rubbing my nose in it – and talked about song-writing ('we can carve Paul's up into twenty pieces,' said Dave. Let's see, twenty by $100, that's 2,000 bucks) and Ringo said it was great to be married, a quote you can read even today. It comes up as fresh as ever.

That evening we had dinner in the open air, along a fine table laid with white linen and silver from a graceful pantry. I was invited with one of those, 'Don't tell a soul, man, just give Dave and Murray the slip, like come alone,' and it was a nice time. Dave and I flew back to LA next day. Bob Eubanks met us at the airport with press photographers, a frown creasing his handsome, suntanned mask. 'Hi buddy. Get the tapes?'

'Yeah man; got the fucking tapes. Lost me soul, tho', lost me soul.'

He seemed very glad to hear it. Gayle and Cecil were waiting back at 6290 Sunset, Joan and the kids were at the airport with Bob and by the time we arrived home in Nichols Canyon, where we had just scored a house before I flew to the Bahamas, I was needed in the office to *write* about my thrilling experiences with the fab Beatles in the sun-drenched Bahamas.

I thought maybe I was really earning the stinking $215 a week and Joan wondered if any money could make up for the changes she was having to go through.

A few days later, Bob Eubanks and his team of mailers, tape-editors and salesmen were ready to market the tapes, segmented, trailered, packaged. Beatlemania would do the rest.

An ad was placed in *Billboard*.

Disaster . . . No one wanted the tapes, at all.

But *these,* we said, were conversations between friends, we said. No deal, said the thundering silence.

And Brian Epstein, through his lawyers in New York, threatened vengeance in the worst way.

'I back down,' I told Bob.

'You stay where you are,' said Bob.

'We won't have hands to count the money.'

Forget it. I backed down and out of Beatle tapes. Also,

I never had the lust for gold again. Money doesn't talk, it swears* and Hollywood is a town of many temptations.

I left Bob Eubanks a few weeks later, taking with me 2½ per cent of the Byrds who were then grossing a few hundred a month and Paul Revere and the Raiders who had been paying Eubanks $750 a month but who asked me would I take $350 a month on account of they weren't all that well heeled (they were in fact very well heeled), and I may not be able to do the job as well without Bob behind me. OK, OK, I'll take it.

This was the middle of 1965. The Byrds' epoch-making *Tambourine Man* had been released and it had made Number 1 in the US and was about to do the same in Britain. Revere had yet to have a hit, but they were good on stage. The Byrds and Revere were both Columbia Records and they didn't really enjoy each other's music though they shared the same producer, Terry Melcher. Serving them was therefore like walking on a tightrope. It was like pedalling backwards on a one-wheeled cycle with a puncture, body all aching and racked with bennies, between 'Revere: the finest performing group in North America, Oregon's answer to Liverpool', and 'America's best group' which is what I thought about the Byrds then and still do, mostly.

When, later, I picked up the Beach Boys, who also wanted their publicist to write 'best' and 'greatest', it became more a matter for a clever thesaurus than a tired, tired biped with twenty clients and five children.

Paul Revere had probably made more money in the mid-sixties out of performing than any other leader of any

* Bob Dylan.

rock'n'roll band in the world. He is still doing it and Mark Lindsay is still fronting the act and, I must say, they have my admiration. They will not quit. The dreams of glory have died, buried above ground by the underground, but the dollar is a dollar, however it is earned, and Paul Revere is not about to call it a day simply because he didn't become a world star. He will live off middle-America until his knees buckle, and why not? They are his people and they owe him something for having him peel potatoes in an asylum for the years of his youth when his religion kept him out of the lousy marines. Whatever break Paul scores from the silent majority, he has paid his dues. Do you know anyone in America who is not paying dues? Well, do you?

We worked together two and a half years and Revere and I must've written close on 175,000 words for him in that time, for the likes of *Flip* magazine and *Teen Life* and *Tiger Beat* and *Teen* and *16*.

Financially, Joan and I swung from branch to branch in those days. We were sometimes awfully hard up. I took up offers of columns in *Tiger Beat*, *Disc* and *Teen*, well paid, offering snippets of news and forecasts. Clean, honest opinions and views made up the bulk of it and in this way I was able to drop in the names of clients who weren't making any waves with their music. It was the dying days of hype.

A sample:

Onwards and upwards rises Percy Sledge, the most exciting new voice of 1966.

Unknown, unheralded, bereft of publicity, this 21-year-old negro from Alabama has stormed through the nation's charts because he possesses the two vital ingredients of a recording artist – a marvellous voice and excellent material.

'When a Man Loves a Woman', his first ever record, will be Number 1 within two weeks and on the strength of it, he has already been booked for two of the biggest rock'n'roll events of the year – the Beach Boys' 'Summer Spectaculars' at the prestigious Cow Palace in San Francisco and the Hollywood Bowl.

Both of these venues are well known to the Beatles: they have played them in 1964 and 1965, and for an unknown to be booked there is really something!

Otherwise life jogs along here much as usual with newcomers causing bewilderment to the locked-up minds in Tin Pan Alley.

One such is Danny Hutton whose 'Funny How Love Can Be' was a slow starter in Los Angeles and now emerges at Number 9 in the city after only two weeks of release.

Despite the Beatles, American ears are not as receptive to new sounds as one would like.

There is a group called 'Love' here with Burt Bacharach's 'My Little Red Book', who are still floundering in the 90s in the national chart – simply because the raw, hard sound of the group is not readily acceptable to teenage ears.

The Byrds sustain their mystical image: 250 people turned out to see them near their hometown on Saturday last week; yet in Houston, Texas, 25,000 fans surged into an auditorium to battle with police for thirty minutes of Byrd music.

The Mindbenders have made it to Number 1 – as expected, as forecast and as they deserve.

Their achievement has had two negative results: it has removed Percy Sledge from the top spot after only one week, and it also keeps the Stones waiting at Number 2 with 'Paint It Black'.

Poor Stones – delayed by the Troggs in England and by the Mindbenders here.

Ironical that two minor-league groups should tackle a giant and win, however briefly.

The Troggs' 'Wild Thing' record, incidentally, is on the air here already – we like it very much. It will be a hit.

So, too, will 'Hungry', Paul Revere and the Raiders' next American release. I think this is the one the group need to demonstrate to British fans what it is they have that has set America aglow with love for them and alive with excitement whenever they appear.

'Hungry' is written by Cynthia Weil and Barry Mann – 'You've Lost That Loving Feeling', 'We Gotta Get Out of This Place' and many other major hits.

Epstein's Cyrkle are doing pretty well. That's an understatement – they're doing *very* well. Number 19 in *Billboard* and *Cashbox* this week (week ending June 11). Well done.

They are in Hollywood this week – opening at the Whisky à Go Go. Much interest in this visit because little is known of the group's background or image and because they had an enormous local hit here with 'Gloria', later covered by a US group called the Shadows of Knight who made it a nationwide chart success.

The Byrds took me into their office and until the man from the tax came for me in 1967, spring, I worked out of there, the eighth floor at 9000. In the beginning my share of the premises was a small room and my share of the staff was half of the secretary, Jackie, who was with me from beginning to end in America and still has scars she can never show to prove that any of it happened.

There was a large room set aside for the Byrds to use for rehearsals. As they never had any rehearsals, they never used it, but David Crosby brought some friends in from San Francisco, and *they* used it. They were nice young people, poor as poor can be. They handed out buttons which said Jefferson Airplane Loves You. They rehearsed every night. Did it show? Does it ever!

There were two managers for the Byrds in those days, long ago. They were Jim Dickson and Eddie Tickner, very clever, delightful men. Dickson was a bald, fair, tall, round man, once married to the actress Diane Varsi. Eddie Tickner was a dark, thin man, more than six feet tall, from Philadelphia. They had a publishing company, Tickson Music, and in 1964 with David Crosby, Jim McGuinn, and Gene Clark they planned the Byrds so completely that it almost happened as planned. They planned to become a big international group without telling any lies, without selling out, and without dropping any of their bizarre friends to meet the pressures of the music industry, then still unused to long hair and madness.

Where the plan failed was that people just cannot get along with each other unless something gives. The Byrds weren't prepared to give way to each other, so they split up and what happens? You get the Byrds and Crosby Stills Nash and Young and The Flying Burrito Brothers and you get Gene Clark in one of his many disguises, each of them as charming as each other and I dare say that by the time you read this, David Crosby will have taken another walk to see what lies further out, still further out, and like, how far out can you get?

In 1965 Jim and Eddie and I were very pleased with each other. The 2 per cent was earning me something like $250 a week, and they had 20 per cent between them, plus publishing from Tickson Music, and even if none of us had had a dime, we would still have been glad to be alive to stand in the wings at Ciro's on the Strip, digging the Byrds. In the summer of that year Billy James was Columbia publicist, Terry Melcher was producer, sales were fantastic, 'Turn! Turn! Turn!' was going to be released (it took seventy takes to get it right, but who but me was counting?), and memories of the dreadful British tour were overlaid with stardust drifting down from the Hollywood Hills.

The Byrds were very good in Britain, but were less than well received. Like every decent group in the 1970s, they tuned up for five/seven minutes (but this was 1965, and the English then were not too patient or hip) and they didn't smile (the British never were that cool – groups were expected to smile even if the audience didn't). The Byrds were the first American group to 'make it' after the Beatles, and the Stones and Dave Clark and Herman and all that lot had 'invaded America'. Motown, loved then only by their own close and discerning group of supporters, had done a tour which flopped, the Beach Boys hadn't yet captured the British, the Airplane was still rehearsing in the 9000 building in LA, there was no UK experience of the Grateful Dead or their friends, nor, really, was there anything American to hang in with so, in their curious way, the British, though fascinated by the obvious quality of the Byrds, also resented the possibility that the American music imported to Britain by the Beatles, might be planning to return home, even if only for a vacation.

In those days, and the more I write, the further off and the further out they become (remember the McGuinn glasses and David Crosby's cape?) – in those days there was the Beatles and everyone else and as we flew to Britain, Michael Clarke, Byrd drummer, was asking, did I figure they would get to meet the Beatles? Since 'These Are Not Merely Interviews, These Are Conversations Between Friends', the last thing I wanted to do was run into the Beatles! Yet, all the pre-publicity to the tour suggested that the Beatles would be intrigued to see what the Byrds were like. So a meeting was unavoidable.

On our first night in London, I stayed in the hotel, the Europa in Grosvenor Square. Mike went out with Gene and David (I think they all went out) and at about 4 a.m. Mike woke me and said, 'We met them, we actually got to meet the Beatles. Paul said "hi" and George wants to see you.' Oh yeah?

Next night it happened that George and John came to Blaises where the Byrds performed to a room no bigger than the one you're sitting in now, on a stage insufficient to carry all the drum kit. They played louder than anyone else had been known to play, even in Madison Square Garden they were bloody loud, and Blaises or blazes, they were going to tune up and belt the music out. I thought they were marvellous and I think John and George did, but some of the English smirkers smirked and you only need a few English smirkers in a half-lit room to feel pleased you're not proud to be English.

Upstairs in Blaises, after the set, John and George sat at a long table and invited us in. Boy, were they big-time then – I'd forgotten. It wasn't them at all, it was the situation. They were absolutely IT. John sat at the centre of the table, George at the head and they sent for wine for free. It came and we arrived with it. 'Thanks for the tapes,' said John, very loud. 'Which tapes?' I said, very soft. 'You know which tapes,' said John, still very loud. 'True,' I said, a little louder, knowing that was the end of that. So it was. We all left, again in that under-the-breath 'come alone' way, John grabbing bottles of wine to wave goodbye by way of goodbye to Jim Carter-Fea, then owner of Blaises, By Appointment, Host to the Beatles.

We went round to Brian Jones's apartment where we smoked some hash and some grass and as there was no food in the place and, after the wine had finished, no liquid excepting a half-bottle of milk, solid as chalk, we went out for hamburgers and then went home.

The Byrds' itinerary in England involved them in thirty concerts in thirteen nights, so you can see they were quite busy. Mike Clarke was the drummer and until time cured him of it, he was a Beatlemaniac. All of the Byrds turned to (were turned on to) rock'n'roll by *A Hard Day's Night*, by seeing that hard rock could have style. Up to then, I guess Crosby and McGuinn were not too moved by it. Crosby was a folknik; McGuinn, greatly intrigued by electronics, jet planes and other manifestations of advanced technology, was also more attuned to folk clubs than to the milieu of the Beatles and Stones.

Anyway, to return to Mike Clarke; he was not well on the British tour and at the BBC one afternoon, rolling over and over with simulated agony, ignored by Crosby, rejected by the others, he decided to do what Ringo did in *A Hard Day's Night*, and minutes before the final run-through of their act, he took a walk and vanished, just like in the movie. He returned – believe it if you will – one second before the live television show started and it was that sort of thing throughout the British trip – all the time, aggro, and panic. The Byrds were bitterly disappointed and so were the press, but there was enough substance in them and in their music for the image not to be blown completely and right now they retain a mystique which fits them well because they are very mysterious.

When they returned to America, I plugged away at their friendship with the Beatles, emphasising their social significance as the first long-haired American group, their triumph in the British and American charts ('Tambourine Man' was Columbia's first US Number 1 for two and a half years, not since Steve & Eydie had that now quite progressive label hit the top) and after 'Turn! Turn! Turn!' consolidated their US success, they became a very highly paid band. But they were certainly going through some changes and first Gene split, then David, and it was only McGuinn's massive inner strength that gave him the fortitude to regroup and insist that the Byrds survive after Chris Hillman and Mike Clarke decided that they, too, had had enough.

We worshipped the Byrds very much, Joan and I, and there has never been anything to touch us with quite so much magic as the first line-up singing their hits on Sunset Boulevard in the mid-sixties. If the Beatles began 'it', then the Byrds too began their 'it' and it is to Roger McGuinn and his four errant, elegant, brilliant friends that we and you, us, and the American nation and young people should offer a nod of thanks for nudging us, and not so slightly, in a new and better direction. It was the end of the age of innocence in rock.

They offered us something very special in those tentative days when, though the peace movement was a baby and LBJ hadn't yet blown it, we knew that there were insufficient options open to the young and free in America. They offered us a maypole around which we could dance. And what dancers! Their timing, their eccentric ('Oh Susanna', 'We'll Meet Again') streak, their great love of what was then folk but isn't now, their chemistry as performers, the tensions, the danger that they might bomb (a danger felt, as much, maybe more, by the audience than by the band, which was saying something), their real musical skill, I mean real, and the alternative lifestyle which they were very early to embody, all of these made the Byrds special.

And they *were* the Beatles' favourite group, they really were, in the days when the Beatles were not so free with their endorsements. And they did give us so many fine offshoots, Burritos, CSN & Y, Dillard & Clark, all of these, and there is still a Byrds. Thank you, thank you, all of you.

One time, when the Good Citizens of Los Angeles, leading or being led by Sheriff Peter Pitchess and Chief William Parker, decided that there were too many young people on Sunset Strip, the Byrds' manager, Jim Dickson, started an organisation called CAFF – Community Action for Fact and Freedom, with headquarters in our offices. First meeting, someone picked my watch (a gorgeous Lucien Piccard gold with the workings also in gold, exposed, has anyone seen it recently?) but I guess the Burrito Bros were right when they sang 'Never carry more than you can eat'. I don't miss the watch any more. I know what the time is. It is later than it was.

CAFF was to subsidise, maybe pay for, the defence and (maybe) fines of kids framed by the law enforcement agencies, to pay for progandising the innocence of the young who hung out on the Strip, and it was the most logical thing in the world that it should have been Dickson who became involved politically, for it was Dickson who had first seen that the Byrds could not be just a rock'n'roll band, but also the musical representatives of a whole sub-culture, unrelated to what was passing for the American Way of Life and its many unfulfilled Dreams.

He organised a concert (Byrds, Buffalo Springfield, Peter, Paul & Mary), a couple of marches and a lot of noise, and though the repression was swift, heavily backed by realtors, restaurateurs, acted out by cops, endorsed by the judiciary and (largely) supported by the media, it brought the whole rotten issue of the Old v the Young into the open and, eventually, curfew enforcement and the harassments of the kids grew less and less, at least in Hollywood.

At the height of the conflict things were tough. I saw my first police 'flying wedge' on Sunset Boulevard, saw how professional cops can always crush amateur freedomniks if they have a mind to, saw a sheriff's deputy spit on a woman, saw Peter Fonda in handcuffs, saw how bad things could be before they got worse, like now.

Those were the middle years, 1965–7, when up north in San Francisco, the Haight was rising, declining and falling from grace, when the peace movement was building, when the death of John Kennedy was really being felt and when Robert Kennedy had not yet been called to declare himself; when, finally, the young realised that it was not the Reds who were doing it to them, but their own parents. From all over the world came a call for change, and rock'n'roll bands everywhere decided to say it with music.

So, having 'dropped out', and having seen how the taxman increasingly directed my cash to war, I looked around for Social Commitment and found it in, of all places, Ben Shapiro's living-room, at breakfast with Ben and Alan Pariser, when we decided to have a pop music festival at Monterey.

6 / About 1965–70 – written 1970.
Danny

Danny Hutton is one of the three members of Three Dog Night, a very fine group with a most special approach to songs. The sound is very pure and musical and they are making a lot of money with it, as one always knew Danny would. When I worked for him we had two things going for us: 1, he had a moustache and 2, he was going to make it.

On this basis, I agreed to accept 5 per cent of his earnings in return for publicising him and Danny and I had two fine years during which he earned, I dare say $2,000, so you can work out my take. He paid it promptly. We had lots of pix taken and some of them got placed, but like Captain Beefheart, Danny was all soul and no fame in those days and the only spread I got him was in *Teen Screen* magazine which ran a page: DANNY'S HAIRY PROBLEM, should he or should he not have a moustache? So you believe what I am about to say: that in 1966 Danny Hutton was the only man in 'new' music to have a moustache. The *only* one? Well, he was. It was a source of much aggravation.

I was introduced to Danny Hutton by a man called Larry Goldberg, a plump and extraordinary managerial guy with a finger in this and that. He signed artists to Hanna-Barbera when that label was funded in millions from the successful cartoon division on which the H-B fortunes were based. Don

Bohanan, then fresh from Liberty Records, was the head of Hanna-Barbera and Larry suggested I go over there, up Cahuenga Boulevard, sweeping through the San Fernando dustbowl, to meet Danny and also the Guilloteens from Memphis, whom I also signed. For an hour or more, Danny's moustache was discussed, but nothing was resolved. Bohanan was for having it off there and then. Goldberg wasn't sure. We must meet later, he said. It would have to be decided, but not without much more conversation. Jesus. Danny said, 'fuck it', 'it was staying'. We didn't then know the phrase 'do your own thing' – only years later did it become a cliché. We took life much more seriously then; thank God we've dropped out of *that* trip, since.

So, after long and troublesome dialogues, we decided to put Danny's hairy problem where it belonged: with the people. They resolved it – moustaches don't make it. They were, and not for the first time, being silly. Still . . . look what happened with moustaches after that. It isn't important, but remember . . . Danny Hutton was first. He doesn't have one now. But Dan Rowan did later. Is there a moral here? I doubt it.

I forgot to mention that, when Danny left Hanna-Barbera, left MGM, went to Dunhill and began to get himself together, he dropped into my office and said, 'About that 5 per cent, I want you to carry on having it, whatever.' Abe Somer, his lawyer, however . . . (I forgive you Abe), Abe said, 'Over my dead body.' Well, anyway, I don't have 5 per cent and now Danny and I can be real friends. He is now very rich and famous and grown up. He means what he is doing. So do all the rock crowd.

What about the others?

So here is Engelbert Humperdinck, if you like, and his story is classic showbiz. He is a man of not much formal education and, insofar as the press have communicated his aesthetic progress to us, he is still less than scholarly. His real name is Gerry Dorsey and in show-business terms, he was a loser for most of his early career. His voice is 'mediocre', his appearance is 'flash' and he styles himself Engelbert Humperdinck, which is a weird trip, yes? He is very rich and he is very popular and he is very nice to his fans and I dare say he has been very nice to his mother. He looks clean and healthy and young; he tries and strives and yearns to be one of the all-time greats of show-business which in itself is not going to get him into the kingdom of heaven, but what the hell, who is to say Engelbert Humperdinck should not be given love and respect for his efforts and who among us can say he had ever been *forced* to watch Engelbert and who can say one word about this man which does not apply in some respect or other to ourselves?

Is it not the case that those such as Engelbert, the ungroovy, the unhip, the uncool, the mediocrities in our multi-talented world of pop, would not exchange all that they have for just one of the gifts of Bob Dylan? Yet to have what Dylan has is to *be* Dylan, and to be Dylan is to have *been* Dylan in the darker years, to have paid his dues, been born in his place, and this is not an option available to anyone but Dylan.

For Dylan read George Harrison, for Humperdinck read anyone. Both lists, the hip and the unhip, are endless and it is not the people on the lists who draw them up, it is the rest of us, and if we ourselves do not wish to be on anyone's list, then we should not be making our own. Turn on, tune in and drop out, writers and critics who prophesy with your pens, keep your eyes open, the chance won't come again.

68

7 / About 1967 – written 1970.
Jerry (excuse me, but are you sane?)

At lunch one time in early 1968, Jerry Moss asked me if I was sane. He said, 'Can I ask you a personal question?' and I said, 'Yes, Jerry,' and then he said, 'Hey, Derek. Don't know quite how to say it, but are you sane, man?' I said I certainly was, 'Yes, *sir*, I'm sane's the day I was born.' He said, 'Hope you didn't mind my asking?' and I said, 'Anytime, man, anytime.'

And then I think, maybe he's got something. Maybe I'm not. So I say, 'Course, I might not be the right man to tell ya. Maybe I'm not sane. How would I know?' He looks kinda frightened. It has gotten real heavy, right? Like, here we are talking about whether one of us is sane. 'Look, I'm not a doctor, Jerry. And you're not, so where do we go from here?' 'I don't want to make a big thing of it,' he exclaims!

Well, listen Jerry, what I say is I think everything's gonna be all right. 'A drink?' he offers. Some more Chablis. Glad to say they had great Chablis at the La Brea Inn. They made a lot of money out of Chablis. I don't mind. (The Inn burnt down in 1970.) Jerry hints some people are worried about me, like it's not *him* . . . but . . . oh, forget it. Nice to have you at A&M records. Jerry is the 'M' of A&M. Herb Alpert is the 'A'.

That was a tough moment. Lunch is over and I don't think Jerry and I ever had any aggro before or after that, but it was tough all the same. Sane, man? Who's sane?

I was at A&M Records for a year, near enough a year. Loved it. Towards the end, knowing I'd have to leave for A is for Apple, B is for Beatles, I would sit on a high stool in a little window overlooking the yard and smoke a joint and talk into a tape-machine, and comment on the passing parade, 'Here's Herb, and there's Bill the Guard with his gun. Hey Bungalow, what didja kill?' It was great material, really stoned, but tight and just as it happened. *Cashbox* (one of the three American music trade magazines) printed some of it. It had a good feel. The whole place had a good feel if you didn't mind that the guard was armed; also they didn't like hair too much in them days. It's all changed now, A&M never stayed the same after it really took off. Growth. Jesus, it had growth! All the way from Chris Montez to Alex Sanders, King of the Witches, to Carole King and Cheech and Chong. All in ten years.

Jerry and Herb made a *home* for music there, sometimes against their better judgements I know. I know how they felt. It didn't come easy to a straight fellow like Jerry Moss, like . . . having known-dope-fiends around, but, to give him his due, he changed too and grew bigger. He is a gentleman and he forced himself so to remain when it wasn't easy. Once he told me he'd heard that one of our guests was a pusherman. 'Well, listen, he's not doing business here.' 'OK, OK. It's your lot. You own it.' Paranoia, you are a *hard* one to live with, that's for sure.

There were three running A&M then. Jerry, Herb and Gil Friesen. They made many millions and they certainly put out some product.

Gil Friesen is a very turned-on young man. When I first

met him he had about four million problems; he had a lot of shoes and people misunderstood him. They gave him shit when he asked for love. Well, look at him now. Did he make it? Yeah. A&M is a great company. What was wrong with Gil in the mid-sixties was what was wrong with lots of us in the mid-sixties – we were uptight. We were on the make and it was killing us, pilling us, and we had no place to go but up, and up was really very down. I met Herb first in 1965 when I had a gig working the West Coast for a magazine called *Record Beat* which closed down, like *Cheetah* closed and *Eye* closed and Liverpool's *Music Echo* closed and God knows how, man. It is a very great tribute to Jann Wenner that he kept *Rolling Stone* together. It is very, very tough launching a new journal and as for making it pay, forget it. Jann was working for *Ramparts* when I ran into him for the first time. Alan Pariser and I had flown to San Francisco from LA to find out what the oracles, like the *Oracle* and all the alternative papers, Wenner, Ralph Gleason and all the hippies and diggers and freaks and all, thought about the Monterey Festival. The word was that them being from San Francisco and us being from Los Angeles – the land of tinsel, false idols and broken promises, we were going to have a hard time convincing them we were honest, and a hard time we had, though not with Jann who was most encouraging and quite (for him) modest. One thing he did lay on us was that we ought to hire the Miller Blues Band for the show, and we did. We were very amiable people.

Had a much harder time with Ralph Gleason, described in the festival book as the trench-coated-conscience of San Francisco rock, and such is his stance and it is for real. He *does* care. He is a very fierce and gifted defender of the faith that he has always had in the power of music to work for good and he was very uptight, at first, about the bringing to Northern California of a Los Angeles-oriented pop festival. He was, as he explained, not about to endorse in the SF *Chronicle* something crude and exploitative of the burgeoning 'Movement'. Like, he didn't want a Flowerpower Festival promoted and hyped and skimmed by Victor Vagina Associates of Sunset Boulevard.

Ben Shapiro, who had asked Alan and me to square Gleason, told us before we flew to San Francisco that if he was against us we could forget the festival. I was also uptight at having to tell an honest man that I was also honest, like what *is* this, what do I have to prove? Who the hell is Ralph Gleason? Shapiro, however, was right. Without Gleason, no deal. Alan and I met him in Enrico's, sitting with his wife and a soft drink. Alan wore his heart on his sleeve (hey Ralph, man, dig, we really want to do a beautiful festival), I wore mine in my mouth. I didn't think he believed a word of what we said; though we should have been convincing, we weren't. Though we told truth, we were from LA! The main objection, as I recall it, was that Alan and Ben stood to make a profit and I was making a nice ($50 a week) salary out of promotion. Gleason said the SF scene was very pure, as pure as it could be given that everyone got some spin-off. But he didn't like all that gold going to Ben Shapiro.

'Judgement reserved,' Gleason more or less said, 'let me know how it shapes up and I'll let you know.' We asked him to be patient and then we all went off to see Martha and the Vandellas and I bumped into Bill Rau, whom I usually try to avoid.

When Ben, Alan and I went in to bat against Gleason, Paul Simon and Art Garfunkel also decided to play, they hurled down some really mean balls and Ben was finally laid out flat. The festival became a charity trip with artists appearing free, workers (HQ staff excepted) doing it for love, and the profits expected to be half a million bucks, to go to some situation where youth and music coincided – guitar classes in a ghetto for instance, which is where the money went.

Ben Shapiro was bought out for five grand and he left with a smile on his face and hate in his heart. Alan Pariser was made co-producer. It was a fine festival and Ben Shapiro turned up with his wife Mickey for the last night and, I guess, they enjoyed themselves. I hope so. Don't forget that the idea of having it was Pariser's and Shapiro's nurtured in Shapiro's house and even if he wasn't to be allowed to finish it, let's now hear it for Ben for trying. For, in the end, all roads pointed to Woodstock, and anyone who helped to erect a signpost to that hallowed spot deserves a smile, a prayer and a song.

We had a hell of a press situation at Monterey. We had 1,100 people who said they were media and we allowed them all in, all! The result was that it was the best covered pop event in history and another result was that, for the first time, the straight press had to realise that there was another sort of press with credentials just as valid as their own enplasticated IDs – the press off the street with a very expanded consciousness. Throughout the festival, we worked out of the badge room where the great and the near great and the nobodies called to get badged. I wrote a piece about the badge room. It went like this:

THE BLOODLESS BATTLE OF THE BADGE

The clean young man at the window said he was from the *Los Angeles Times* and there was nothing in his face to say he wasn't, except that we know he wasn't because if he had been, Pete Johnson who was, would have said as well. Pete Johnson tells you when he is going to tie his shoelace or comb his hair and he wouldn't have forgotten to mention another *LA Times* man.

The man at the window said he needed a press badge and he's heard that I'm the man for press badges. Well I was the man for press badges but was he the man who needed a badge, we asked ourselves and then him. Credentials? We asked from the badge side of the window and from the badge-less side he said gee it was lousy but he'd left everything back in the motel.

It was the Monterey International Pop Festival and in the badge room we were paying the fees for triumph. There were 60,000 people in and out of the fair and fervent festival of music, love and flowers and it seemed 1,000 of them were journalists. At any rate in the open-badgehanded first two days we'd issued 1,000 press badges. Purple.

Unfortunately, the accommodation in the press section in the concert arena was built for 250 people in faint discomfort, for 400 at a crush, for 600 in civilian prison condition, for 800 in boot-camp circumstances, and for 1,000 only in Buchenwald terms.

On Sunday, the third day, I made the most melancholy announcement of the joyous weekend over the speaker system: 'The line it is drawn, the curse it is cast. The purple press badge is now invalid. Come to the press room for your new badge.'

The line it was drawn all right, and the line it was formed anew with purple badge holders waiting to be re-validated with a new emblem of access. Green.

The man from the *Los Angeles Times* reconstructed the lines on his face to a freshly sincere mask and we said: 'Ask your city desk to call and it will be OK.' 'How do I get them to call?' he asked and we said, 'Call them.' 'Oh,' he said, and vanished.

'Photog,' said the next man who had many curls. Credentials? 'Yeah,' he said, lumping out a wallet which contained a two-inch square copy of a cover-girl picture from a magazine. 'Not enough,' we said. True. Any other credentials apart from an unsubstantiated last name and an uncredited picture from a magazine? 'Yes,' he said and pulled out a driving ticket. 'Your man is there,' we said, pointing to a passing highway patrolman. The man ducked and said, 'There's a warrant for me,' and dropped his wallet. Two obscene pictures fell out and we didn't see him again.

A wire service was next. Crew-cutted, toad-skinned, veteran of countless murders, untold fires, limitless acts of violence, one too many wars. 'Working press,' he said wearily, looking at our psychedelics, our buttons, bows, balls and scarves like Alice through the Looking-glass. 'When did it cease being a pleasure?' we asked. 'A long time ago, buddy,' said the wire service, re-folding a yard of credentials. 'You can weed out this gang. There's not a working press among them.' You don't say.

'*Pool News*,' said a nervous mouth in a young and grubby face. 'What's *Pool News*?' we asked and the mouth growing paler said: 'A rock'n'roll magazine. It's sold all over the world.' Why was it called '*Pool News*' if it was about rock'n'roll? Why is *Time Magazine* called *Time*?' she responded, not without anger. 'Because that's what it's about,' we said. 'No pass. Sorry.' 'Schmuck,' said *Pool News* and meant it.

Richard DiLello, hippy holder of two purple badges, no credentials and no money, came to the window with *UPI*, the *Village Voice* and a photographer from *Time Magazine* who had been thrown out of the arena the night before. 'Sorry, Richard,' we said. 'Badges are rationed.' He went without complaint. *UPI* unrolled the plastic. 'OK?' he said. 'Need any more?' 'Working press,' he added, as by rote. 'When did it cease being a pleasure?' No reply. The *Village Voice* said could it come in and speak? Of course. *Time Magazine* was still angry and wanted to know what I had meant the night before when I said his problem was trivial in relation to the overall success of the festival. I said that what I'd meant was that his problem was trivial to the overall success of the festival and he said he could see how that was one way of looking at it. Very generous I thought and apologised for appearing rude. Appearing?

The window darkened with a flurry of hair and bearded and beaded literate hippies from Haight-Ashbury and Sunset Strip. The *LA Oracle*, the *Berkely Barb*, the *San Francisco Oracle*, the *Los Angeles Free Press*.

Two for each paper, we said. Now man, said the Underground press. We're your friends. We're all on the same side. Well, that's true. But two each. Take their names, Carol.

The Haight-Ashbury paper said only two? Well, yes. But there are three of us. Well, if Haight-Ashbury doesn't know how to share two badges between three people then Haight hasn't yet come to terms with Ashbury. 'Fair,' said Haight-Ashbury and it was.

Mac Bowe was at the window. Working press he said,

folding his face and unfolding his credentials. Are you the Mac Bowe who said it was a marijuana festival? Why, he said, does that mean I don't get a badge? Oh no, we said, but come in for a chat. Mac Bowe came in and said he had discovered some very obscene buttons. What, he said, do you think of a button stating 'Reagan eats it'? I don't know what it means, I said. Well, he said, all this drugs and LSD. It's wrong. What LSD? we said. I don't need it, he said three times. No, we said, you don't need it. Poor Mac, he spent the entire festival spotting dirty buttons, ferreting out lewd news-papers, sniffing around for pot and when, finally, the festival had totally succeeded, he followed through as he had begun with the conclusion: 'No more pop festivals for Monterey.' As he said: 'I'm not here for fun.'

KRLA Radio arrived for eight badges. Seven they had names for: the eighth was for someone Jim Steack their spokesman couldn't remember. 'Your girl-friend, maybe, Jim?' Seven badges, Carol, for KRLA. One for Jim Steack's girl-friend. Blush, thanks.

A cloaked photographer, high as high as high as and on the very best grass smiled an eternal blessing and was instantly awarded badge of the month. He, being unable to talk, smiled a thanks and returned minutes later with a girl simi-larly loaded. 'Isn't she beautiful. Beautiful. Just beautiful?' 'Yes.' A badge for her. Green. As grass.

Are the Beatles here? asked the *San Francisco Examiner*. No, we said, later saying yes when the question re-arose, yes being a more acceptable answer than no in most circum-stances. Yes the Beatles are here, disguised as hippies. A cheerful rumour which resulted in an additional one thou-sand people in the arena that night.

Look Magazine came to the window and went with badges.

So did *Flip*, *Soul*, *Tiger Beat*, *Hit Parader* and *Teen Scoop*, bedrock of the fanmags . . . The window saw one thousand people that last day of the festival. At dusk as the Mamas and the Papas – whose John Phillips had, with their producer Lou Adler, mounted the most successful multiple event in the history of pop (newly claiming recognition as an art form) music – as this group of groups prepared for the final concert, at dusk we placed on the window a notice which read: 'We thank the Press and Radio for their selfless interest in this festival of music and people and regret that there are no more pieces of paper to – them.'

We walked the *Time* and *Life* men to the arena and gave them special places in the wings; we crushed a final grabbing arm in the lowered window, we said good night and goodbye to the window itself and it was amazing and wonderful to know that beyond the badges, far from the pass-system, over and above the demands, there was a festival.

It happened in Monterey and it mightn't have done.

Joan was pregnant with our fifth child but she flew in for the first night with the four we had. I went down to Monterey Airport to meet her. She was on the same flight with the Animals and lotsanlotsof fine freaks. What a trip it all was. Every plane skimming low over the Pacific bright with fresh cargoes of acid-heads and amps and coats of many colours. Up there in the festival grounds it was like the greatest show on earth, all life and vigour and health and loud, loud music. It was good to be, it was good to be. There were hassles, but they were about nothing and no one. The Chief of Police said it had been like a dream and we gave him a necklace. There wasn't one arrest and there wasn't one injury and the Mayor said she was very pleased with the young people who had come to her city. Music, love and flowers . . . the motto had come true and next year the city, remembering, decided such a thing must not happen again, and it hasn't since – not in Monterey. But once, it did happen in Monterey, a long time ago.

8 / About 1966 – written 1970.
The woman in white

Well then, David Mallet called me one day in Hollywood and asked me if I would like to represent Mae West, I said, oh I don't know, I'm very busy, you know how it is. He said she had made a rock'n'roll record, an album called *Way Out West* for Tower Records (a Capitol subsidiary which Capitol closed with an axe in the back in 1969), and she was going to need publicity on account of she had not been heard of for some years.

David Mallet was then in his early twenties. He was British, living in Hollywood, and working as assistant producer to Jack Good on *Shindig!*, and like Jack he was very enthusiastic and persuasive and it took him all of half a minute to persuade me to change my mind and I promised to work for Miss West.

He warned me there was much to be done. 'She is a very fussy old lady,' he said, 'but you mustn't ever use the word "old" in her presence. She would be very cross, very cross indeed. I will talk to her about you – I have already broached the subject – and then you must come to see her and she must be able to look at you and weigh you up.'

I waited for a day or two and he called me again and said, 'Miss West is still deciding whether she needs a press agent.' A week later, he again called me and said, 'Miss West still doesn't know what to do for the best but she has consented to meet you and it will be entirely up to you, it will depend entirely on your attitude as to whether she hires you. She is a very fussy old lady, but you must never use . . .'

'I know, I must never use the word "old" in her presence.' David said the appointment was for three o'clock in the afternoon two days later.

Now, in those days I had a little grey suit which I had bought from His Clothes in Carnaby Street at the end of 1964 to accommodate my shrinking body, having lost a stone in the service of the Beatles. It was a nice little suit. It was very neat and compact, and it was the sort of suit you could wear at a school prizegiving and have mothers say you looked very smart.

I put on a white cotton shirt and a black James Bond knitted silk tie and black leather shoes and the little grey suit and a little drink and a little pill and then I caught a yellow cab to old Hollywood, down below Vine Street, and I was in very good time for my appointment when I reached the lobby at the old and very baroque apartment block where Miss West lived and had lived since the high days of Hollywood.

I announced myself to the lady behind the desk and I heard her pass my name to Miss West. 'I have Mr Taylor wishing to visit with you,' and then I went upstairs by elevator. I think it was wrought iron, but that may only be a quirk of memory. I rang the bell at her door and wished I had remembered to go to the bathroom. David Mallet answered the door and let me in. 'Hello,' he whispered, 'Miss West is not quite ready. Do come in.'

We went into a long white room. Clearly, it was Mae

West's. There was a nude painting of her set upon the white grand piano and there were photographs of her in furs, and it was a very nice room. I was very nervous. David sat on my left, and we waited in almost total silence, exchanging only whispered comments on how absolutely fantastic the room was and what a fine (old) lady she must be, as if we were being taped or eavesdropped.

I watched the door through which David had said she would enter, waiting for the big blonde star of all our memories to sashay through it, filling the room with sex and power and wit.

Instead, a sweet little old lady walked in, wearing a long white satin gown, and a tumbling wig of pale gold and a very knowing smile. David jumped up and I stood, grinning as suavely as I knew, to be introduced as Mr Taylor from England, The Man We Have Been Talking About.

A conversation began, on general topics, like music and weather and how are you and she was very nice but as nervous as we were and I think we were all relieved when she produced some props so that we could relate to something other than each other.

The props were fan letters from young men who had gotten themselves involved with a Mae West cult which at that time (1965–6) was very small and in no way pointing to the cover of *Life* magazine and *Myra Breckinridge* and all that was to follow. She was proud as hell of the letters because they told her she was still the greatest and though she was rich, richer than ever, and though her retirement had been voluntary, and though she was still in the best of health and not obviously seeking any renewal of past glories, she was nevertheless a star in need of recognition, appreciation, love, even?

We read the letters and she told us about the old days when instead of hundreds a month, there were tens of thousands a week, and she amazed us when she said she had only made half a dozen films in her entire career. Half a dozen? Is that all it had taken to make her the greatest?

Well, not really because as she said, she had been the biggest thing on Broadway for scores of years, taking her own train to tour with her plays. She said she wrote the plays and cast them and if they had succeeded it was because of her and of course there is no disputing that and who would want to? In the hands of a woman like Mae, ego becomes a very precious jewel for which modesty would be a most unbecoming setting.

She said that she had been taught ever since she was a tiny child to think and behave like a star. Her mother, she said, had told her that when she stepped out of her clothes, she was to walk away from them. 'Somebody else would always pick them up,' mother said, and she was right. Someone else always did.

Mae said she had never taken alcohol and all her life she had been opposed to tobacco, ever since her father, Battling Jack West, a prizefighter for whom she had the greatest affection, had upset her child's sensibilities by breathing the heavy stench of Havanas over her.

David had warned me about smoking and on each visit I excused myself from the drawing-room and removed myself to Mae's bathroom where I opened the window and belted through half a Marlboro in four minutes, watched closely by her fluffy ivory négligée. I hoped it couldn't speak. It looked so like Mae it was surprising it didn't speak.

In days gone by, she said, she had been careful to prepare for the future which was why, now, she felt able to participate. 'I was never in a hurry to make a decision. If I was buying land' – she has a lot of very valuable real estate in Los Angeles – 'I would go for a drive with a friend and I would see a corner of land and I would ask my friend to investigate was it for sale, what would it realise in ten years, things like that. I would like to know for myself what I was getting into. That way I could know what was going on.' Her close identification, her ventures landed her in gaol once, in New York in the play *Sex*, which she wrote for herself. Sentenced to a week and a day, or thereabouts, for obscenity, she survived not only the scandal (how could she have failed?), but also the rigours of being locked up for she was such a favourite that in the evenings gaolers would take turns to drive her around Manhattan for 'a break in the routine' before returning her to her cell and, even in gaol, she stepped out of her clothes and someone else picked them up.

After my first meeting with Mae, David said, 'She likes you. It's on.'

The fee was $300 for a month and the aim was to make Mae a rock'n'roll star.

I went up to see her again, and then again and much of the time I spent listening to tales of old, she didn't like the (then new) topless craze, she said, because it didn't hide anything. 'In my day,' she explained, 'it was suggested, lightly, with style and humour. We didn't just display them and say, "Look, here they are."'

She said it upset her to drive along Sunset Boulevard and see so much blatant titillation. 'You should do that sort of thing with class, with understatement.' Mae said that her leading men enjoyed working with her because she gave them a dignity which was lacking in the second half of this twentieth century. 'I chose my men because they had class,' she said, 'and I let them keep it and use it in my films.'

Cary Grant she had spotted walking across the lot in the early thirties. 'I said to the man who was with me, who *is* that fine young man, so masculine the way he walks. I was *very* impressed. You can appreciate how he must have looked in those days. So I put him in my picture and he has done very well, hasn't he?'

Mae was obsessed with Self. I am not complaining about it. It would be silly to expect anything else. Seventy years in show-business, mostly at the centre of adoring throngs, out-stretched arms, hemkissing; nice work if you can get it but it doesn't make good listeners. She was very funny though and she told terribly good stories. She said she had never made a cup of coffee in her life; there was always someone around who was good at that sort of thing. The way she saw it, the gal who invented the shimmy didn't need to make coffee as well. One day, she said, one day quite recently, she said, she had been alone in the apartment and she had thought to her-self, 'Well, I most certainly would like to drink a good cup of coffee right now.' The more she thought about it the more she wanted a good cup of coffee and at length she could wait no longer and she telephoned the very nice young man in the lobby and asked him how she should make coffee. He told her how to place the grains in the top of the percolator and fill the thing with water and place it on the electric stove and turn the switch from left to right. She said that she did all this and settled down to watch it. After some time the pot began to boil, and then it began to hiss and spit and spurt the bubble and jolt and jerk and rock and roll and she became very frightened, she said, so she phoned the nice young man in the lobby and she said that the coffee was certainly going to explode, what should she *do*? The nice young man said: 'The switch on the electric stove, you know the one.' 'Uh huh.' 'Well, you must turn it from right to left and then the problem will be solved. As a precaution, however, you should first remove the pot from the heat.'

'I was so relieved,' Mae said. 'Such a clever young man. I should never have thought to do that.'

Mostly, in the days I was visiting her, we were waited upon by a stocky quiet friendly chap named Paul Novak, a companion of Mae's for many a year.

He brought us coca-cola and orange juice and all of that and I would've loved something stronger but rules were rules and if Paul Novak had any whisky around the place he certainly kept it well hidden. Well, one day while Paul was around the corner Mae launched into a tale about a guy who had written to her boasting of an extraordinary sexual feat and the room became very warm and the interviewer with me (Danny Fields, one of the few great music business freaks from out of the mid-sixties) and I were wondering was it true, Mae West was really getting down to some basic talk . . .?

No. She ended the story in the middle abruptly and indicated she was tired, shook our hands and retired most graciously and I never saw her again. By the time I reached my office her secretary had called to say that Miss West and I had enjoyed a satisfactory and useful relationship which was now complete and a cheque would follow.

The cheque did follow; I xeroxed it, cashed it, lost the xerox and Bob's your uncle. End of short story and au revoir Mae; you're still the greatest.

9 / About 1968 – written 1971.
The long and winding road: Annabel

On 22 March 1969, Annabel Lucie Taylor was born.

It happened like this.

In April 1968, Neil Aspinall and John Lennon and Paul McCartney and I were sitting in Nat Weiss's apartment in New York talking about nothing at all. On Nat's record player Paul played a brass band-style version of 'Thingumy-bob', a tune he had written for a television series of the same name which was one of the magnificent line-up programmes with which the new London Weekend Television company was planning to open its first season and justify its manifesto of great promise.

The version was very ordinary. I was very stoned. I said: 'Seems to me the only way to get a brass band sound on a gramophone record, is to use a brass band.' The best band in the *land*,' said Paul. Yes.

Now in those days there was never a long wait between the musical will and the recorded deed and by phone the best band in the land was swiftly found, hired and asked to report to the Victoria Hall, Saltaire, Bradford, a fine Northern location for a brass band, at ten o'clock on Sunday morning, a fine Northern time of day for a brass band. We flew back to England.

Joan and I lived then in Newdigate, Surrey. 'Laudate' was a beautiful little Japanese house overlooking a lake on eleven acres of land; house and land owned and leased to us by Peter Asher. It was an acid-head's dream down there and many dreams we had in the twilight of that long psychedelic idyll of the late sixties.

The house had the strangest vibrations. I don't think there was a day we didn't feel we knew for sure without actually knowing anything for sure, that we were being watched by odd men and funny women.

The only others on the land were the monocled man who cared for the estate, his wife and their children. They lived in a caravan nearby, in two caravans in fact. She communed with animals and birds and was further out than she knew. At 4.15 a.m. in a thunderstorm she walked into a trip involving John, Neil, and Pete Shotton, Joan and me. When I say walked in, I mean *walked in* out of the darkness, sliding open the glass door on the lakeside of the house, pulling aside the curtain and bang! there she stood on our trip with an enormous armful of damp washing. 'Nearly got soaked,' she said, laughing like a maniac.

John was very taken with her. She said she too sang. It was now four-thirty in the morning, and we were getting higher and higher. The suspension of disbelief: she said she would write a song there and then about what was going on. She did too: John gazed at her in wonder. He told her she could make an album and paint the cover herself.

At 5 a.m. she left and the vibration changed and we became afraid. Who else was out there? Terror. Just terror.

No need to worry. It was only Chief Superintendent Tommy Butler and his avengers waiting for Bruce Reynolds (remember the train robbers?) to come back. (This we learned but not till much later in 1968 long after we had left the house and come to the Gables, safe in golfing Surrey, away from the bats and owls of Newdigate. Only a manhunt for Bruce Reynolds. The Japanese house where we dared to explore our madness was where he had dared to explore his freedom before moving to Torquay where Chief Superintendent Butler nabbed him not long before he himself was nabbed by cancer and taken off in a wooden overcoat by the Reaper to do the sort of Bird that God stores up for career-coppers who live with their mothers.)

Laudate had always been very freaky. Aristocratic homosexuals had romped there drinking gin and lacing the lake with toilet rolls and getting their naughty names in the *News of the World*. At other times Peter Scott had come to watch wildfowl, and in grimmer days Peter Louis Alphon had told all to Jean Justice, the lawyer who still fights to prove Hanratty didn't do it.

At Laudate in Newdigate I decided that Saturday to take a very modest 250 milligrams of LSD in a final cup of tea with Joan before setting off for St John's Wood to pick up Paul McCartney and Peter Asher and Tony Bramwell, the Apple team due next day at Bradford.

A fine black Rolls arrived and I was packed and ready for a rolling trip of medium duration, minimal strength and maximum visuals for there is nothing like a ride in a Rolls on a little acid on a Saturday afternoon in June in the lanes of Surrey.

And so it turned out. Paul seemed very positive and played us some rare recordings; 'dubs' he had made of songs, written by him for others, dubs on which he was singing for the first and last time. Maybe one day they will make an album of them, but maybe it will have to be over his dead body for I don't see him wishing to complete that particular symphony in his lifetime.

I said I had taken a dollop of the dreaded heaven-and-hell, and Paul said it should be an interesting journey, and it was. We stopped at a pub on the way up and I astonished myself by coping remarkably well up until the point where I asked the barman if I could buy a filthy table which stood in a corner covered in cigarette burns and the stains of long-dead pints.

He said, 'What would you want with an old thing like that, better to get a new one.' It hadn't been anything special even when it *was* new, he told us. 'You may not believe this,' I replied, 'but it is the cigarette burns and the stains I am really buying. They are so incredibly far out.'

'Drink up,' said Paul, seeing the signs and playing Dad. 'Write your name here please, Paul,' said the barman and we left.

We arrived in Bradford after dark. Some disabled people were operating rowing machines in a charity marathon in a local showroom. We wandered in and looked, leaving some silver in the collecting boxes, neither the first nor the last of the small spenders.

It was midnight as we checked into the hotel. There wasn't a soul or a sound except for the red-nosed night porter, as old as Moses. Paul had brought Martha (My Dear) with him – the sheepdog of the same name. 'Can you shampoo her?' he asked the porter who recoiled in terror. 'It's her arse,' said Paul, and he put his fingers in the thick curls around Martha's back passage and pulled off a cluster of clinkers.

'Look!' I nearly fainted. 'I'm afraid not,' said the porter. It was very late after all.

Next morning, another lovely day. I felt very nice and clean around the brain, always have a lovely morning after acid. A few months earlier Paul and I had gone shopping for suits; he had told me navy blue pinstripe was already on the way back (meaning that he wore it) and I fell for it – and ordered one.

I had taken it with me to Bradford; just right for Bradford I said. I wore it down to breakfast and then we went off to the Victoria Hall where the Black Dyke Mills Band were waiting on hard wooden chairs, looking bloody marvellous and real and solid and honourable and stocky and lots of other words like that. Paul had on a magenta shirt and a white jacket, double breasted, with black trousers (no one had ever told him they were on the way back), and the Black Dyke Mills Band was quite stunned by his charm and by the way he handled the music.

Marvellous recordings were made, indoors and later in the street, of both 'Thingumybob' and 'Yellow Submarine'. It was a good morning for everyone because the portable recording unit worked, the band and McCartney worked, and the press worked out beautifully – I saw dozens of old friends and we had a few pints and then lunch.

At around three o'clock, as we filmed the last TV interview ('How do you like Bradford?' 'It's great . . .'; fast-moving stuff like that) I decided to off the suit and black shoes, put on a pair of red corduroys and a white Mexican cotton shirt from Olvera Street, Los Angeles, a couple of beads, an Indian scarf and down my throat went another 250 milligrams of the dreaded heaven-and-hell drug. What a day for a daydream.

'Should be an interesting journey,' said Paul.

The chauffeur said: 'Back to London?' and we said 'yes', not sure that it was the right answer.

Alan Smith of the *New Musical Express*, Alan who had been on the *Birkenhead News* when I was on the *Liverpool Daily Post*, was travelling back with us and was taping interviews; so lively the journey became and, asked about Biafra, Paul said he had to confess, he didn't really care about Biafra, if he had he would have gone there, wouldn't he?

Smith: 'Really?'

McCartney: 'Own up! Who really cares about anyone else?' And so on.

As we rolled away from the South Midlands and approached the Northern Home Counties the acid really started to bounce. It was late afternoon and if there was a heaven to be found on this soil, then I reckoned it would be found this evening, in the green and gold of this divine countryside.

'Would you like to swing on a star, carry moonbeams home in a jar?' 'Yes,' said Peter Asher. 'Where would you like to go?' I asked. 'AA Book,' said Paul. 'Pick the most beautiful name in Bedfordshire,' I said, 'that's where we should go.'

Peter looked at the map for what seemed like two hours or more.

'Harrold,' he said, after fifteen seconds.

'Harrold?' said the driver, naturally knocked out with delight to leave the M1 and crawl down B, C and D roads to a village no one in the car, including himself, had ever heard of. We wound through Bedfordshire checking off the signs steadily until we reached the village sign: Harrold. Oh, it was a joyful Sunday sight.

It was *the* village we were supposed to have fought the world wars to defend, for which we would be expected to fight the third when told to, but won't. It was a Miniver hamlet on the Ouse and there were notices telling of the fete next Saturday, and a war memorial which made me weep. Thrushes and blackbirds sang and swallows dived into thatches and a little old mower wheezed as we walked down the only street there was past the inn which was closed, past the church which was open, nodding to a sandy man with a 1930s moustache and khaki shorts as he clipped his hedge and stared at these city people with funny hair and clothes.

It was seven o'clock and acid or no acid, it was opening time and I steered us into the most beautiful village inn the world has ever known and there were three or four people in there, or more or less; magical antique villagers with smocks and shepherd's crooks and also there was a fruit machine offering Jolly Joker tokens. Through the dancing lights, past the sparkle of the green and tawny bottles, I saw the sandy man with the khaki shorts.

I went to the Jolly Joker and stared at him as he spun past, parallel lines of leering jokers circling the globe, mocking my greed, never stopping at the same time, matching with lemons, cherries, apples, half a striped plum, never the Jokers met to jackpot me into the problem of cashing twenty jokers behind a bar which now seemed a thousand miles away behind the sandy man and his knowing smile.

'Welcome to Harrold, Paul,' said the sandy man, the local dentist, downing the rich gold beer he had earned with his shears. 'I can hardly believe it, in fact I think I'm dreaming.'

We next found ourselves in his house, below dipping oak

94

beams, a banquet provided for us, hams and pies and multi-jewelled salads, new bread and cakes, chicken and fruit and wine; and the dentist's wife, a jolly lady, still young beyond her maddest fantasies, bringing out her finest fare. Paul McCartney was at her table in the village of Harrold.

Hiding at a turn on the crooked staircase stood a little girl, shy and disbelieving. But she had brought a right-handed guitar and landed it in Paul's (left-handed) hands but the wizards were producing this play by now and floating with the splendour of this, the strangest Happening since Harrold was born, the dentist and his wife, and the neighbours as they crowded the windows and the parlour, and the children, all caught their breath as Paul McCartney began to play the song he had written that week: 'Hey Jude,' it began.

I sat peacefully, full of the goodness you can find within yourself when goodness is all around and the dentist's wife picked up on it and asked why life couldn't always be like this and I told her there was nothing to fear, nothing at all and the dentist brought out the wine he had been saving for the raffle at the fete next Saturday and we drank that to celebrate the death of fear and the coming of music to Harrold and then, and gradually, the dentist was freaking and he asked me what I thought I was talking about and for a moment it was very tough, very. Ah, but Dr Leary's medicine was good that day and we came back to a good position again, but I didn't feel quite right about the dentist after that, and I don't think he felt quite right about me, but how was he to know and what was I to do? You don't just tell strangers you've been taking that naughty old heaven'n'hell drug.

It was now eleven o'clock and we were still in the house

and the inn was closed but a winged messenger came to say that as this was the night of nights, never to return, the inn was to be re-opened. 'In *your* honour, Paul.'

It was 11 p.m. Paul had The Look on his face, the 'do we don't we?' I nodded: tonight we should. The pub was absolutely full. The whole village was here. Paul played the piano until at three o'clock a woman stood and sang 'The Fool on the Hill' and he left the piano to dance with her and kiss her on the cheek and then I went and sat in the little garden and cried for joy that we had come to Harrold. It was a most beautiful garden, with hundreds of old-fashioned flowers, lupins, foxgloves – that sort of thing, and Alan Smith came out, pissed as a newt and said, 'Why so sad, old friend, why so sad on such a night?' 'Not sad,' I said, 'not sad, old pal, just happy to be alive.'

We left then, waved away by the Harrolds, by all of them, and we never went back and I never looked at the map again, not even to see if Harrold was there.

It was full of day and birds and dancing daisies at Laudate as I tiptoed over the rush matting in the little Japanese house, into the bedroom as Joan opened her eyes and smiled. 'Hello, darling,' full of sleep, 'had a good time?'

As best I could, I told her what I have told you and because she has been somewhere like that herself, she understood and put out her arms and I slipped into bed and what with one thing and another, Annabel Lucie Taylor was born on 22 March in the following year.

And it happened like that.

The word is that the press are going to massacre Apple which is a big deal. Ray Coleman who edits *Disc and Music Echo* tells me 'the knives are out', which is another big deal. Jeremy Pascall from *Rave* and *Nineteen* magazine tells me he only wants the truth.

Don Short from the *Daily Mirror* says Dougie Marlborough of the *Daily Mail* really has it in for Apple, for the Beatles and for me. Bob Barr of the Westinghouse Broadcasting Co. says he has no respect for the British press. Lucinda Franks promises me that UPI will carry a more favourable story than AP. Allan Hall of the *Sun* says George Harrison is not the man he used to be. Five reporters from the *Daily Express* conclude that the Apple has gone sour and quote the company's leading competitor in support of their conclusion. Ho ho. The *Evening News* says that the Rolling Stones have a greater sense of responsibility than the Beatles. *The People* has secured an exclusive interview with Brian Epstein, taped by Ivor Novello and shipped through a medium in West Hampstead. Anne Nightingale from the *Daily Sketch* wishes she hadn't been in Tunisia when the anti-Beatle storm broke. She would have written something nice about them. The *Liverpool Daily Post* hopes the Beatles haven't forgotten their humble beginnings; the *Western Mail,* Cardiff hopes

Mary Hopkin hasn't forgotten hers. The *Sunday Mirror* believes John Lennon to be in Austria. The *Evening Standard* wants some facts; Stella from the *Daily Telegraph* doesn't know 'anything about pop music'.* 'What's Donovan's first name?' she asks. 'How do you spell Angelo, Michael?' Phillip Palmer of *Record Retailer* wants to share the Beatles' financial secrets. Bill Harry of Liverpool wants the boys to play the Cavern again. Bill Marshall of the *Daily Mirror* doesn't want the Derek Taylor to change. Tony Barrow of NEMS doesn't want to comment. I don't want to die. The BBC doesn't want to know. *Melody Maker* just needs something for the front page.

Time Out would like an advertisement for *Wonderwall* as they're good enough to review it this month. *Record Retailer* would like an ad just for being there. The *Sunday Times* would like to be congratulated for staying away. The *Sun* would like to be forgiven for rising, and the rain would like to be forgiven for falling. Every day has a life of its own, and the press marks time. For us who live in black and in grey the only white is in our children's eyes.

World at One wonders what's happening? *Scene and Heard* thinks Ringo has the answer to the Beatles' image. *Nova* wants Yoko to approve the article. *Look* magazine won't let Yoko approve theirs. *Fabulous* magazine is no longer Fabulous, and *Petticoat*'s readers no longer wear them. *Private Eye* went public. I would like to go private. So what on earth am I doing writing all this down? I must be crazy. I am crazy. And so are you. And so are they. So it's OK.

* She later learned plenty. She is a fan now.

11 / About 1968–70 – written 1972.
A brave building in a fussy street

The Apple building is in Savile Row, a street which believes itself to be awfully important. It lies behind Regent Street, another street which has a high opinion of itself. Both are in the Western End of London, glamorised some time between the wars by the title 'West End', a phrase much affected by the media to suggest a beautiful way of life in which big band leaders and rich society people wined and dined and opined on the really essential things like oysters and quails and champagne and staying up late and keeping things much the way they are, only better and bigger and finer.

Savile Row didn't really welcome the Beatles. Many of the shopkeepers there, silly, snobbish, growly, obsequious people, believed that since they had been selling marvellous suits to marvellous people they had a right to be the *only* ones there which is about as daft as you can get, for, as Lewis Carroll said, a cat *may* look at a king, though few enough choose to. When the Beatles gave their wonderful rooftop concert and, however briefly, gave West London a shining hour of absolutely unique excitement, in 1969, it was the stiffnecked shits of Savile Row who called in the law and had the music stopped.

Anyway, the Apple building *is* in Savile Row and it doesn't look like going away although if the scaffolding were taken down there is no absolute guarantee that it wouldn't collapse in a heap of eighteenth-century bricks.*

Apple was in Wigmore Street, London, first as a temporary measure, and I decided to move out first, long before Savile Row was properly ready. Wigmore Street was really awful. It was occupied mostly by office people, strapped into suits and ties and we were forever getting stoned in the evenings and finding ourselves locked in by those people whose delight is in locking and bolting doors and running to the pub for a fix of firewater and ice, and fuck anyone who's locked in. I went over to Savile Row one morning and never returned to Wigmore Street. We sat on a plank, my secretary and I, and old pal Richard came over and we set up shop and prepared for the premiere of the movie *Yellow Submarine* which meant really that we hired some fancy clothes and resisted requests for interviews and carried out other little tasks.

Neil Aspinall had found Number Three Savile Row and as it only cost half a million pounds it seemed like a bargain. It had five storeys and a basement where Magic Alex built a studio which was later ripped out and replaced by another. Magic Alex was Alexis Mardas, a blond and handsome Greek with a terribly serious face and a dazzling smile. He arrived in England knowing only two people – Mick Jagger and the Duke of Edinburgh. He met the Beatles in the acid summer and that was that and that was that and *that* was that.

He could do anything, make any fantasy come true. His plans were many and more and more amazing; to make a force-field round a house and fill it with coloured air so that

---

* The staff are now in St James's while builders spend a couple of years making sure that Number Three, Savile Row, *doesn't* collapse.

no one could get in (it didn't matter because no one got hurt and the colour was good); to put a noise *in* a record, inaudible *on* a record but so nasty that when anyone tried to tape the record the noise would be reproduced as an appalling scream; to invent a telephone so sensitive that you would tell it who to ring – just say to it 'ring the king' and it would; to make a few changes to a car so that it would illuminate from behind when anyone got too close; to invent a camera which would take pictures through people's walls and see what they were up to . . . and of course there was a recording studio to build and a dream to fulfil and a world to change.

Well, well, well . . . not much happened but if Alex Mardas wasn't magic then why was he called Magic Alex? There must have been something so wherever you are Alex, you are magic . . . yes, you are.

In the beginning Number Three was very untogether and so were we, though a doorman was found and a receptionist for the ground floor. I had the main ground-floor office – being first I made sure I scored it – but I later gave it up to Ron Kass, head of Apple Records and Apple Music who was subsequently upended, shaken out and rudely treated by Allen Klein, and then John took the room over and made it a centre for more fine madness than I had ever known, or ever will again. I moved to the second floor and Neil and Peter Brown took the first. The Beatles were to set up their own room, like a cheerful millionaire's commune but that never came to anything because they were getting deeper into the eternity of business meetings and horror shows which led, finally, to the High Court and which have not, even now, four years later, shown any real signs of solution. The accountants were given the usual choice of the worst rooms; at the top of the building, Peter Asher was planning the career of James Taylor and others who would come running to sign with Apple:

Date   1st June 1968
From   Peter Asher
To   Ron Kass c.c. Neil Aspinall

JAMES TAYLOR: He is an American song writer and singer who is extremely good. He wrote Tom Rush's last single and several tracks on Tom Rush's album. He and I have found a bass player and a pianist with whom he is currently rehearsing a dozen or so of his own songs. They seem to be coming out very well because he knows exactly what he wants and both the musicians with him are very competent.

We intend to start recording him about the 20th June, by which time he will have enough songs rehearsed and arranged with me. He is ready to discuss contracts and things as soon as you are.

I have a demo tape of his in the office should you want to hear him.

Apple should also try to get his publishing, but you probably know more about this than me.

Peter Brown was personal assistant to the Beatles, best man to Paul and to John at their weddings, fixer supreme, tremendously smooth. He had been Brian's personal assistant and before that he had worked in big stores. For a provincial boy, Peter was very impressive and he ran grand lunches in his grand room, and I must say it was a lot of pleasure to be eating good meals and fresh vegetables and drinking Chateau En Gerryfitt and Remy Martin Bormann in the late sixties. We were allowed, even encouraged, to plan our own decorations.

Mine was a hotchpotch of colour and artifacts and nonsense with a tiny desk and a vast white cane chair of the sort now much affected by models advertising cigars or tits or vaginal deodorants. I brought it home when I left Apple and the left arm rest is bent and broken where I leaned so many long, long hours listening to as many hardluck stories as time and tempers would allow.

Neil Aspinall's room was a high-class Headorama full of visuals, with a lovely fireplace and chimney corner. Neil has always been with the Beatles; maybe he can remember when he wasn't but I can't. He is a fine man, began as the road manager, became managing director of Apple and was deposed by Klein but allowed to remain, if allowed is the word, but it isn't. Neil *had* to remain because he is Neil. It is impossible to explain so I won't.

If you want to speak to Neil, ring Apple. He could make a great movie, create beautiful pictures, do anything, but so far he hasn't. Not one the public has seen, anyway. One day I hope he will. One day I hope you will see his work. The Beatles, however, cast a tall shadow and a wide one. It is not their fault – they have given 'breaks' galore but what is a break? What we all need is not breaks but challenge.

Mal Evans (Neil's companion when they were managing the road before the job got its own title and its own dignity and its truly fascinating place in the complexities of touring, in other words before we heard the word 'roadies'), is still at Apple and still one of the greatest roadies the world has ever known. But more than any of us he found a way to adapt to changing times and he became a record producer (Badfinger), played parts in movies *(Help, Magical Mystery Tour, Blindman* with Ringo and others) and he is willing to serve if he may and there is nothing nobler than real service I believe.

Apple had a kitchen of its own and we were always told that the cooks were Cordon Bleu and I think they were. They were very nice posh girls, with good legs. I think they, too, have gone, but I can never be sure. After Peter left to become an impresario and present *JC Superstar* for Robert Stigwood on Broadway, the accountants moved into his room and others moved into mine when I joined Warner's and now the Creatives are in the holes and corners and the Adding Machines have the rooms with the fireplaces and the brass chimney seats. The more things change, the more they are not the same any more.

We published two magazines while I was with Apple, both very free and honest which, more than anything, showed that we were an experiment in business operations, that we were fresh and we were green, and when they said we were rotten and going broke, they were wrong. We were not. We were going right. All we wanted was more consistency and a visionary with a business brain at the top (rather than four visionaries growing up and apart painfully and publicly). We should have relaxed more. We had plenty of money (Apple never did go broke), and we had plenty of gifted people working there or offering to work with us. We were very short of time and we began to panic. The acid and the pot and my independence with my own clients and, much more than this, the Californian experience had not prepared me for administrative life back in Britain. Life on the open road hadn't prepared Neil for life behind a desk, talking to cold crude bankers with the accents of Eton and the minds of hyenas.

But we tried and we did wonderfully well at times. The Beatles themselves made the White Album and *Let It Be* and *Abbey Road* and *Yellow Submarine* was released. John met Yoko and Paul met Linda and George became a producer and Ringo (never mind the reviews) made two movies which he enjoyed making and two albums which he had always wanted to make; all of this happened during the first three years of Apple. Mary Hopkin was found, launched and she made it whatever you may think of her music – she came out of Wales and brought a lot of freshness into middle of the road entertainment, Badfinger had a home where they could sit it out while they were broke waiting to make it, James Taylor made an excellent first album, Doris Troy and Billy Preston had a crack at whatever they cared to do and tens of thousands of the good and the bad, the ugly and the beautiful could always drop in and make their pitch or pitch their tent, be they Ken Kesey or Harry Nilsson or Harold Wilson. There was always some baby brew from a big brass cup or a rest on a big brass bed or a big brass handout or a big brass band at Apple in the sixties, so, in the end, who's counting the cost except the accountants and for Christ'sake, they and the lawyers have little enough to complain about about Apple. They doin' fine man.

ABSALOM, BOLLOCKS, PROFIT & MOTIVE LTD

1046–7 New Ponce Street, Mayfair, London, W1

D. W. Taylor Esq.
Apple Corps,
3 Savile Row,
London W. 1

Dear Mr Taylor,

Pleased to have made your acquaintance before the holiday, albeit across a beer rather than a desk. I think my company is in an invidious position. From what you say, practically everyone that walks through your door has the solution to Apple's problem. We have not. What we do have is a mechanism for the objective appraisal of such problems. This mechanism can rather accurately measure the difference between what is being achieved and what could be achieved in a given commercial situation. Needless to say, this operation is carried out in a professional manner in complete confidence and with the minimum disruption to the operation under study. We are then able to recommend one of three courses of action:

(a) The provision of a fully documented action programme for implementation by the client's staff.

(b) Where the client's own staff have neither sufficient time and/or know-how, a quotation for our own specialists to implement the recommendations. Or,

(c) A reasoned amalgam of (a) and (b) – this is frequently the more realistic approach.

I am led to believe that Mr Aspinall, your Managing Director, has been appraised of our services, agrees in principle, but must have the sanction of at least one Beatle before going ahead. Please get a Beatle's ear. Or better, get me a Beatle's ear. Let us resolve this before Apple has spent another surreptitious £10,000. In our favour, three points:

1. As a company we are newcomers, although the team is greatly experienced, as a company we are less than twelve months old. You will not be 'just another client'.

2. Being new we are still flexible, an essential ingredient when optimising profits in a climate of 'controlled weirdness' (*sic* P. McCartney, *Observer*, 6 April).

3. The appraisal we recommend is purely diagnostic. It changes nothing but proposes corrective action which may or may not meet with the clients' acceptance.

It will take our organisation a maximum of ten days to assemble the appropriate team. I confirm the initial cost at 450 gns to cover the expenses incurred and that this is your only obligation under our standard Terms of Agreement, two copies of which are enclosed.

For your information, Mr Ken Absalom is no longer with us and the writer would be grateful if you would contact him

107

direct should any further amplification be required, and if you want a meeting outside normal office hours, with a little notice, we can oblige.

Yours, etc.

Funnily enough it was the Mr Absalom of the last paragraph who had made the first approach. The straight world and its strange emissaries with their strained game-playing faces and gins and optimised profits *(sic)* frequently came into Apple but rarely reached the second floor. Businessmen found our room little to their immediate liking – it was poorly lit by ICI IBM CIA standards, the posters of Satan, half-dressed naughty nuns and Jimi Hendrix were a lot to take if you were selling reorganisational procedures or million-pound endowment policies, and the music and the incense could be very distracting – but those who did allow themselves to be lulled by a tumbler of Bell's whisky and great bowlsful of patience and courtesy (for we were anything but hostile unless challenged by extremes of the freak or straight communities), would usually allow that we were certainly 'different' and they would leave, murmuring that it must be nice to work in such a place 'for a time'.

I don't know where they thought any of *us* had come from. Some, I know, put it all down to 'drugs' and 'working for the Beatles'. For myself freaking went back twenty years or more to the army. The Education Centre at Durranhill Heavy Ack Ack camp had been much the same. Wits and wags in the Sergeants' mess had called it the Golden Slipper Club, such a compliment.

Well, it was Mr Absalom who came first on behalf of Absalom, Bollocks, Profit & Motive. He was a Scot, not above thirty-five and quite decent in a smirking, public school sort of way. We met in a pub near Apple, a horrible hole of a place, stuffed with grey and navy suits with endlessly deep trouser pockets knuckled by nervous change-jangling business hands, the air raucous with boasts, dry guffaws and spluttered punchlines from dirty jokes left over from the fifties.

Mr Absalom said he made the approach after a meeting his company had held as a result of what they had read in the *Observer*. He and his company wanted to straighten us out. It was very important that we should be straightened out. We would be absolutely OK when we had been straightened out. When we had been straightened out we would be able to go straight ahead.

Mr Absalom said his father had an estate far from London, land with mountains and mists and salmon streams, and you could walk for miles and never meet another soul and never an enemy, no matter how far you walked.

We had us our gins and I asked him if he missed the countryside. 'For two pins, you know, I would be there now,' he said. 'Still, I've got a jolly challenging job, a young company in a growth market.' Another director, he promised, would be coming to fill me in on any points that might need clearing up.

Mr Absalom was the ice-breaker. He told me it would be remarkably painless getting ourselves straightened out. Let's face it, the Beatles are jolly talented, but running a company wasn't like writing a song.

Mr Bollocks arrived, older than Mr Absalom, harder,

bigger, readier to smile, stronger. A prick. I drank my gin and left. After ten minutes of jolly goods, we'll drop you a line, very nice meeting yous, and very nice meeting yous, I was glad to leave.

Next, the letter arrived. I didn't reply to it.

A couple of weeks later, Mr Absalom arrived, in the lobby at Apple. He sent up a note:

'Sorry to bother you but as you may have heard, I am no longer with Absalom, Bollocks Profit & Motive and I am having rather a tough time. Could you possibly lend me something, say five pounds; I promise faithfully to pay it back tomorrow without fail: Yrs, A. Absalom.'

Sent him a fiver down, went to the bog and sat there for ten minutes. What a world, what a terrible, crazy world. I should be so lucky, and the Beatles too, to be straightened out by Absalom, Bollocks, Profit & Motive.

It was around this time that Allen Klein arrived. As it turned out, some now may take the outrageous view that even Absalom, Profit, Bollocks, Motive and Solomon, with all their stopwatches, could not have disarrayed us more than did Allen Klein in the beginning, and at an inclusive cost of 450 guineas it would have been marginally less expensive than Klein's first month in town.

Now read on.

When Allen Klein came to Apple there were those who feared him and those who didn't fear him. There were those who didn't even think about him, like the cooks and the cleaners and the office boys and the filing people and tea ladies – the essential people who are usually paid less than anyone else

110

and whose absence from work can have a quite appalling and immediate effect on the temper and morale of the highly paid groovers and bossmen whose own absence is frequently very beneficial to the businesses they are supposed to run.

I was very excited when Klein hit town and moved into the Dorchester with his rough tough New York minders. They were a change from the whey-faced English miseries who had offered to sort us all out. Klein came up to see me and said everything was going to be 'great'. Great was a great word in those days. Great.

Klein said he wouldn't upset anything. He would just rearrange it. So I wasn't frightened because I thought that if it was just going to be a rearrangement then that would leave me unmarked since I was always rearranging myself anyway. What I didn't want was to be upset. Who needs upset?

Then the firings began. We had talked about firings many times before and Paul had been talking of them almost since the beginning of Apple. Neil and I were asked not once, not twice, but twice times a hundred or more times to draw up a list of who should stay and who should go, but we never could get round to it. Nor could Paul. Maybe Eichmann could, but he was dead. Maybe Dr Mengele, but he was in Paraguay. Klein's strength was that he didn't need no lists, man, he just needed the figures. Then he could begin to rationalise us.

Klein would meet me on the stairs from time to time and he would say: 'I saw the figures for the last ten years and these guys have been robbed.' I always responded the same way: 'Me?' 'Naw,' he would say, 'your department isn't at all bad.'

It wasn't a very expensive department we had on the

111

second floor. We had no hirecars or hotel bills or nights out in clubs. We had a terrific staff. Lots of us and all nice. We had Mavis, who had worked for Leslie Perrin who is now the PR man for John, George and Ringo, for Apple for the Stones and Sinatra and Lulu and dozens of others. Les is OK. He says he never poaches staff or clients and I say I never poach either and I dare say neither of us poaches. I suppose the salmon just swim up to us and ask to be caught. Mavis is the wife of Alan Smith who used to be on the *Birkenhead News* when I was on the *Hoylake News* in faraway Cheshire. Alan is the Editor of the *New Musical Express* and as we go to press with this book, he is adding readers by the thousand. Good luck Alan and good luck Mavis. Then there was Richard DiLello. Richard is from Forest Hills, New York. He is in his twenties and we met when he was a boy in Los Angeles. Richard was, he would say, a slave. He did everything that needed to be done by someone like him. He was never a slave. He was an author doing tasks for a publicist and both of us were writing books anyway. His will be out around the same time as this. Can't wait to read it. It is about Apple. He told me he had written it about the beginning of 1971 and I badly wanted to read it but he was no fool. I walked him from Bloomsbury, down to Trafalgar Square and along Whitehall to Westminster Bridge one evening on my way to pick up Timothy, my son. We didn't talk too much about the book, Richard and I, not until we had a drink by the House of Commons and then I hit Richard with it: 'Can't I read it?' 'Waal, no,' he said. He wrote me a year later, from New York. The letter said he was a failure, that he had been rejected by every publisher in the USA.

Then he called me a few weeks later, early in 1972, and said *Playboy* has bought the book for a lot of money. Serial rights, hard and soft cover and all. He is in England, he says, and he came to visit the office and we smoked a lot and he came to the house and we climbed mountains of conversation and I am really thrilled and delighted he has a book out. He says it is called *The Longest Cocktail Party*. So it was, too. Quite the longest. Now that it is published he says he is going to write the Brigitte Bardot Story. *Bon chance, mon ami.*

Richard's father and mother ran an Italian restaurant in Queens, New York. They are now retired. I was very proud of Richard, somehow. He is the very best of America.

There was Carol in our Apple room. She was Number One secretary. She nearly lasted longer than any of us. She was with Apple when I joined and she stayed there when I went home into semi-retirement to write this. Then one morning Klein gave Carol and Richard not many hours' notice and not many more pounds and my office was closed down. Mavis had left some months earlier to become a housewife. There were other secretaries and friends working out of the room, Sally who had been a model and Frankie Hart who had arrived with the San Francisco Hells Angels and stayed behind to work for me for free and all the Scotch and tea she could drink. George Harrison stole her for his personal assistant and then she split for San Francisco and she has been with Bob Weir of the Grateful Dead for many a long year since. Saw her this week with Bob. They may marry soon. There was Veronica who came as a temporary and stayed. There was Francie Schwartz for a time; Francie too was an author, and briefly Paul's girl-friend. She would take

113

notes all day and she has a book coming out as well. So much writing talent in one room?

Stocky McMullen was with us for about half a year, he sat mostly on the top of a filing cabinet and drew elaborate fantasy pictures of penises eating each other. He had called me, sight unseen, from London Airport one morning and said he was on a bummer and could he come by. Oh yes, we said, and he did and as I say, he was with us for six months. Richard and Stocky became friends and they shared their tasks – tea-making and so on. Sylvia was another secretary; she came as a temporary, became indispensable and stayed on and off for three years. A girl called Dicken arrived on the second floor one morning with a donkey, a gift from Jeremy Banks, a crazy man who was also with us for nearly half a year, a champagne and aspirin-crazed photographers' agent with a flair for fixing pictures. I brought the donkey home and she is still here. Dicken herself joined Joan and me for a time as a help with the children and animals, so you see, a lot was saved at Apple. It was for people, no doubt about that. How many offices are for people? Not too many.

We were always very busy, we worked very hard and all of us had some talent. Mine was energy. Richard's was intelligence – all the rest of the kids were as bright and attractive as can be and there was no nicer place to visit in all of England in a working day. Anyone will tell you that, except for a few miserable buggers who left without what they'd come for, whatever that was. And no one left without something having been stuck into their mouth be it tea, whisky, cigarette, joint or clenched fist.

That was my Apple, or some of it. When my office closed

and I gave up writing this – I returned to a different Apple. My artifacts and posters and friends had gone, and the room was as smooth as silk, and dead. Really dead. I would sit with Neil in his room and we would get drowsy by the fire and then go out for lunch, for long lunches. Then that too died and I left. Well, well, well. Say what you like. That was what happened and it was all right in the end.

13 / About 1969 – written before
it was too late.
An ABKCO managed company

I work for Apple. Apple is an ABKCO Managed Company, or so the advertisements for Apple tell us. Apple pays me, therefore ABKCO pays me. The head of ABKCO is Allen Klein of New York, New York. Allen Klein is a business-man. He has had dealings with a guy called Tony Calder who worked as a partner for Andrew Oldham. The three of them managed the affairs of the Rolling Stones. Oldham & Calder left the Stones scene, but Klein stayed. Oldham & Calder ran Immediate Records, which went bust. I know Calder and I like him. Calder sees me one morning, a year or so ago (he lives near me; I live in Sunningdale, he lives in the next vil-lage, which is Virginia Water), and he says he will give me a lift to work in his Morgan. I usually go to work by train, but I say 'OK Tony', and I travel to town in his two-seat Morgan with him and his wife. Clearly, there is one too many people in this car, but what the hell. Tony has something on his mind that is why he is taking me to work in his Morgan.

He says: 'Allen Klein says you are in his way. Allen says you are blocking him from meeting the Beatles and doing business with them.'

I am amazed. I say, 'I never give Allen Klein a thought from one year to the next. What is the guy talking about, me being in his way?' Tony says, 'Allen couldn't accept that you don't give him a thought. His ego wouldn't stand it. He thinks he is on everybody's mind all the time.'

I say: 'Too bad.' Tony says: 'Allen thinks you are sore at him because he gave you a verbalising in his office in 1966.' I say: 'He is an asshole for thinking that.'

But true enough, Klein did give me 'a verbalising' in 1966. It happened like this. Andrew Oldham comes into the Gaiety Delicatessen on Sunset Strip where I did a lot of my business in 1966. He takes me from my table to a quieter table. He says: 'Would you like to handle the Stones' press?' I say, I would, because I am a sucker for saying 'Yes' in 1966. He says: 'OK. Come to NY, NY on Saturday and meet the fellers. Also you can meet Klein at the *Sullivan Show* next day and do the deal. What will you want?'

I tell Oldham I'll ask for a thou a month. He looks very pi and I go to NY and I meet the Stones, one or two of whom I half know and we get on like a supermarket on fire. Next day I go to the *Sullivan Show* and there is this short fat man in a seersucker shirt and it is Allen Klein. He comes on very cool, like he knows all about me but he is not going to let it be any big thing. I know he knows I am always short of bread because everyone knows that. I know he knows that I am not short of friends, because everyone knows that, too. I also know that with Klein, bread/friendwise, it is exactly the other way round. I figure that either we will make it together or we will not. There will be no half measures.

We go to a restaurant and I have food and beer. He doesn't drink or smoke at all and he doesn't eat too much either. He is not happy in the restaurant, but I am. It is Sunday afternoon.

117

I am small-talking and he is drumming his fingers. He says: 'Hey, we can't talk here. Let's go to my office, I got a great office.' I don't think that I can think of anything less groovy than going to a Manhattan office on a Sunday afternoon, but it is no good arguing because he isn't going to do any deal in a café, and I have come 3,000 miles to do a deal so it is his call in his town. We go to his office and he sits me opposite him. He is in his big, important chair behind his big, important desk and I am dying of thirst. He is feeling very good, however, and he tells me all about where I should get myself re-motivated, start looking for the real bread, etcetera, why . . . I am wasting my life. I think maybe he is right, so I lay on him that I would like a thousand dollars a month to work the Stones and also I would like to know where is the water cooler. My mouth is dry from pills. I get some water and then some more. He tells me things about how to make money and what sort of a corporate set-up I should need and how he came from nowhere to be a big guy and by the time I leave and he leaves; I don't hear one word about whether I work for the Stones and the fee or any goddam thing that I came to discuss but I think we-ell, maybe he feels better, and it was nice seeing the Stones and I will be home tomorrow so what's it matter apart from I had to leave Joan and the kids on the other side of the sub-continent (and Timothy had broken his arm a day or two before) to come to Allen Klein's 14,000th-floor office in Manhattan.

A few months later he sent me some bread to cover my fare and I didn't give him another thought (didn't get the Stones either) till I was in this Morgan car with Tony Calder three years later, and one hell of a lifetime older and wiser.

So I tell Tony if Klein thinks I am in his way, and as I'm not in his way, I'd better show the guy I'm not, by moving out of the way anyone else who might be in his way.

I tell Tony to tell Klein I am (a) not in his way, and (b) if anyone else is, I will remove them. I tell Tony to tell Klein to call. I go into work at Apple and I see Peter Brown, Brian's old pal, mine, the Beatles, Apple's and so on. Peter knows many things. I say, 'Allen Klein wants to meet the Beatles.' 'Does he ever,' says Peter. I ask: 'Is there anyone in his way?' Peter says, 'Only the Beatles.'

He explains Brian didn't like Klein and the Beatles had never heard anything about him that attracted them either.

I ask him will he take a call from Klein (on account of he is the Beatles' personal assistant, the last filter – or was), and he says he will.

The way is clear and Klein places his call. He doesn't get through, nowhere near does he get, and he must have called Les Perrin who represented Klein because Les calls me and says: 'Klein says he can't reach Peter Brown.' I say I'll check and then I go into lunch with the Beatles in the room opposite Peter's which is now Neil's but was then the Beatles' own, born in a dream and left unfurnished because a dream is just a wish you hope will come true and this one didn't. At lunch it is one of those days, it is like eating toast under water. It is a real down time and they are still talking about how lousy Apple is and how we are a lot of time-serving fools, the usual stuff, you know. I say there is this guy Klein who badly wants to see them. John says yeah, Klein's been trying to reach him but he won't take the call. I do some hype for Klein and say he is a strange cat, hated by some of the people who met him

119

and also by some of the people who have only heard of him. George says, 'he sounds really nice', and I say that if they want someone to run their money scene then Klein may be the man.

But I also say they had better look at him very hard and ask around Jagger and Donovan and the others he handles. I mean *really* check Klein out. But see him too. See him face to face. John says OK, I'll see him and the others rhubarb a bit and that's the lunch over.

I call Les Perrin and tell him tell Klein to call and Klein does and then he flies over really fast, like *yesterday*. He meets John, they talk all night and boy do they dig each other. John comes into the office and says, 'Don't care about the others, don't give a shit . . . but I'm having Klein, he can have all of my stuff and get it sorted out.'

John says there is too much fear around, everyone must stop being frightened, everything is going to be fantastic, like Klein is going to be the genie of the lamp.

Paul, George and Ringo get to meet Klein and he begins to act as if he is half-hired but maybe not. He says he will save Northern Songs from the wicked Lew Grade. He says he will buy NEMS Enterprises. He says he will take EMI to the cleaners. In the end he doesn't save Northern Songs and he doesn't buy NEMS Enterprises, but takes EMI and Capitol to the cleaners and to hell and back, and it is Stanley Gortikov, a senior executive at Capitol, who says a lot later that year that OK, Capitol paid up, but did Klein have to be so hard about it? Capitol, says Gortikov, would have paid up anyway. Would they?

Klein tells George he will get him more money and he tells

Ringo the same. He tells them all that there are four first-class Beatles, not two and John doesn't mind being told this. Paul doesn't like any of it, none of it. He has a father-in-law who is also from New York and his name is Lee Eastman. Lee Eastman is also a toughie, but his manners are more formal than Klein's and some people like him. Paul would like Eastman to be the Mr Big Apple needs. John wants Mr Klein to be Mr Big. A year passes. It is 1970. Paul still doesn't like Klein but John digs him more than ever and George digs him more than that and Ringo doesn't mind him. Paul? He is so uptight about Klein he only leaves the Beatles, that's all.

Klein and me meet the press and TV and all that; together we sit on a sofa and talk about Paul. Mr Klein, why doesn't Paul like you? Mr Taylor, why doesn't Paul like Mr Klein? I don't know, don't ask me, man, don't ask me.

Paul releases his album and Klein releases the Beatles' album and they both make a million and Klein has had Phil Spector remix Paul's song 'The Long and Winding Road', adding a women's choir and some violins etc. Paul thinks this is the shittiest thing anyone has ever done to him and that is saying something, but Klein laughs up his silk sleeve and releases 'Long and Winding Road' as a single anyway and still with Phil's new arrangement. Up there in Scotland, Paul McCartney, one of the four owners of Apple, the company formed to give total freedom, artistic control, to struggling performers and writers, wonders what went wrong, when even *he* can't control his own work. I am wondering too. Everyone is wondering. But Klein isn't wondering. He knows, he knows.

Klein is now Mr Big and Apple is an ABKCO (Allen B.

Klein & Co., get it?) Managed Company. Two dozen people had gone, maybe more. Some invited to go, others have resigned in despair, executives, accountants, beavers, squirrels, pluggers, musicians, gone, gone. There are no more hired cars, no more lunches, no more liquor for guests, workers sign in and out, the laughing is over, the wastage has been stopped, and as John Lennon has said, the circus has left town but the Beatles still own the site.

Money is pouring into Apple so I guess you could say that Allen Klein straightened Apple out as the Beatles wanted it.

The only thing is . . . where is Apple and where are the Beatles? If you find out, please let me know, I haven't seen them in a long time.

The way I see it, Klein is really bringing a whole lot of people down, including me sometimes and I have a deal which keeps me at home writing stuff like this so what am I whining about?

Well, being as how I brought Klein to Apple, by making sure the way was clear, I owe someone, somewhere something, that's for sure.

What is it and what have I done? Our Apple is all chewed up. It is the most ungroovy place I ever knew and I have to say it, we have all let it happen, all of us, but *me*, I told Tony Calder to tell Klein to call and if I am going to make any more mistakes about Allen Klein, then let it be writing this, let it be.

14 / Of 1969 – written then.
Muttu and other mutterings

Tambi Muttu isn't well and the *Evening Standard* wants to know if I approve of Tambi Muttu, who is an Indian, a grey-maned, handsome Indian who has taken everything from acid to vitamin X through an ocean of hard liquor to end up looking good and very cheeky, asking Apple to back a poetry journal. Why not, why not? What is there to lose that you don't have to spare?

However, the question is on ice because Apple don't know whether they want to put money into Tambi's poetry journal and also because Tambi isn't at all well. We told the *Evening Standard* that Apple approved of Tambi, and that also we liked him very much because he was charming and clever and true and went back a long way.

Tambi, I said, was a fine man. The *Standard* wanted to know if Tambi had actually met one of the Beatles. 'Yes, George.' Then he actually did meet George? Yes. Then the *Standard* said, 'thank you' and no doubt felt that Tambi Muttu really *was* a good honourable man now that it was confirmed that he had actually met a Beatle and been approved by the mighty Apple for whom I was spokesman, and becoming a man power-crazed, living on or off a treacherous charm.

Tambi wants to use our Apple trademark for his new magazine, and would also like a desk, a telephone, and the use of

Apple's address for letter-headings and suchlike. Moreover, he would like the money to back the magazine.

Now, though I think Tambi is a great man, the demands are pretty heavy and Apple really has no intention of getting into poetry. Not after the shops closing, not after all of that. God protect us.

So I gave Tambi a comfortable seat at my left elbow and Richard the Hippie kept the drink moving, and from time to time sat with Tambi and vibrated positively and well, so that by and by, Tambi, not knowing whether he was pissed or on a trip, forgot what he had come in for. That pleased us because it meant we didn't have to fork out any money or promises, of the first of which we had little, and of the second of which we had far too many.

Tambi had been for some long time at Millbrook with Timothy Leary and the other blithe spirits who led the way for so many of us potential acid-heads who would have liked to have tried it earlier if only we had the courage. So thanks for the courage, Doctor Leary, we said to ourselves. Your name is not forgotten, old pal.

Tambi looks as if he knows everything in the world but he can't or he wouldn't be so silly.

He was a recent arrival at Apple's talk-salon on the second floor, though as he rambled on it seemed as if he'd been there for years, making his pitch, dreaming his dreams aloud, and good dreams they were; *only* good dreams.

It is not much to ask of life that you should be given money to publish a little monthly book of new poems, is it, I asked myself.

It wasn't as if Tambi was asking for a loan to get him

through four days at Royal Ascot. It was only a little book of poems, I reasoned, and it was because it was only a little book of poems that Tambi was so welcome.

Mister X came to Apple once, from Canada. He was not a nice man. He wanted $30,000 to launch a new concept in retailing furniture. He had short black flat lacquered hair and glasses and from the back his head looked like Rudolf Hess. He wore bell-bottomed purple or green trousers, and carried a briefcase and several grudges. One grudge was that he had been in England five days and no one from Apple would see him. This was conveyed to me by someone in the next phone booth to X's somewhere in Chelsea who was eavesdropping on X and learned that he was planning to do Apple 'some harm'. Dark threat, darkly offered and wilily eavesdropped. I, not anxious for Apple to be harmed, found X and called him up to the throne-room where he created so many instant and bad vibrations that I knocked over a cup of tea.

Mister X said he was from Canada and he had come all the way from Canada and he was not going to be fucked about. No sir. If we were as good as we said we were, and as honest and forward-looking as we said we were, and if we were as groovy and hip as we claimed to be, then, oh boy, we had no alternative but to bankroll Clive X to the tune of thirty grand, yes sir! Do, he said. Well, well, well, we said.

We said it was clearly a trap and faced with the choice of coming off like good honest forward-looking groovy hip guys (and handing over the bread which *said* we were all of those things), and with coming off like shits, I took the latter route and Mr X was quick to tell us we were shits.

I said I would have taken the other route, had I had the 30 gs,

125

but I had only eight shillings and an ounce of hash. Mr X said he was not going to get bogged down by a lot of dumb people who couldn't see what a fine deal he was offering. I said I could sympathise with that. 'You have no intelligence,' he told me and I nodded. 'And you have no honesty,' he said.

This was true, I agreed, inviting Mr X to leave.

'Your vibes are very bad,' I said trendily, 'and you are a cunt.'

Mr X said he would prefer to finish his drink and then find someone with some decency and common sense who could dig his furniture scheme and get the Beatles to hand over the bread. Maybe, too, he would like a ceremony with his own photographer there to capture on film the smiles and handshakes as 'John, Paul, George and Ringo, yes, folks, the Beatles, hand over a cheque for $30,000 to Canada's brilliant Mr X.' Or something of the sort, I thought, reaching for the intercom button.

Mr X sat bolt upright drinking his drink in nervous sips, looking fiercely around the room at a forest of badly vibed heads. He was clearly feeling very good. The negative buzz was flowing like molten honey through his system. The voice of Silly Jimmy came on the intercom. 'Yes?' 'Mr X, who is in my room, wishes to be assisted to leave,' I said. Mr X couldn't have felt better and he smiled broadly and said, 'This is what I suspected,' and I said it was great that he'd found what he'd come for. So many people left Apple disappointed, it was good that he had found what he expected, suspected. He was assisted out, and he looked very like Rudolph Hess as he left the room with Silly Jimmy helping him on his way back to Canada.

126

He gave an interview later, to the *Toronto Globe* and together he and the writer concluded that the Apple was rotten at the core. A few weeks later, Mr X's negative buzz alighted on the negative antenna of a man named Mr Z, also from Canada. Mr Z arrived at Apple, but couldn't get in on account of I had told the receptionist to keep him out because Mr Z generated problems like a fly spreads disease.

Mr Z was a disc jockey and he looked like a hippy and isn't. He liked meeting famous people and asking them questions. That was his kick and we have no comment to make. We all need kicks and we get them where we can. It was just that Z's kick was meeting famous people and asking them questions. It is not strictly classified as insanity but time will tell. Another thing about Mr Z is that not only does he like meeting famous people and asking them questions, but he also gets paid for it. In other words he is an interviewer. Now I reckoned if it was not only this man's kick, but also his sole means of support that he meets famous people and gets to ask them questions, then to deprive him of famous people would be not only to send him out of his mind, but would also be to starve him to death. However, I decided, it was Z's sanity or my own and, on balance, I valued mine more. It was difficult to get Z to see it this way, for the way he saw it, his own needs were bigger than mine. He told me, 'Now listen, I am here to make a film which will tell Canada that X was wrong about Apple'. That must be some film, a *mighty* film that could tell Canada that X was wrong about Apple!

I went into my paranoid state and wondered if there could be anything that mattered less than Apple, or anyone who was more trivial than Z, unless, possibly, it was X.

Z was not allowed in to Apple that day, but he made it later and brought with him all the problems in the world. Well, well, well. Apple sure made itself a field of thistles and a thorn hedge sky-high when it said it was a home for people who needed a break. I helped to spread the word that Apple was willing and thought maybe it was no use trying to blame anyone for Black Friday – the day when Hells Angels, the managers of the Grateful Dead, a homeless family of seven from California, the Beach Boys, Hare Krishna, two transcendental meditators from Rishikesh, Mary Hopkin, George Harrison, John Lennon, Yoko Ono, a German television producer, and Tambi Muttu all arrived at once, needing cups of tea and conversation.

It is over. Black Friday, it is over and I am still alive, and recall few details, few indeed.

The homeless family were homeless no more by the New Year. They had come from the hills beyond Los Angeles, Mick and Annie – husband and wife and five children, barefoot in spirit and very broke. They had tried to reach me many times, once in New York. I had invited them to tea and left the hotel forgetting the invitation. Their aim, they said, was to get Paul McCartney to bankroll them to an island near Fiji, where the sun shines all the time, and also they planned on Paul travelling with them. They told me I should also prepare for the journey, without delay, with my wife and children. No time must be lost. An emissary had landed on these shores two months before Mick and Annie.

Tall and fair with a pale silk dress down to her sandal-feet, belled and chained, she arrived one afternoon in Paul's yard; she came over the gate and began to cry. She had to see Paul because Mick and Annie ('Annie *was* the Lady Madonna of the song, wasn't she?' the courier sobbed into the soft folds of her dress) were on their way and time was short, oh so short. Well, Paul was busy what with one album or another, and Fiji would have to wait, I said and not unkindly. Mick and Annie hit Apple near Christmas and I gave them the third floor waiting room until they found a home. Determination pays off and it wasn't any time at all before the homeless family from California had found their island, not in Fiji after all but off Ireland, and not just any old island, but John Lennon's and it was theirs, theirs alone and if that ain't a dream come true, I never had a dream.

Time magazine wondered whether the Beatles had any comment on J. S. Bach and *Newsweek* wanted to know what the Beatles wanted for Christmas. I wanted to know what the Beatles had to do with either Bach or Christmas, and the Beatles didn't want to know about anything, and me not blaming them, I sat at my desk and seeing once again the lined and smiling face of Tambi Muttu in the room, did no more useful work that day, remembering on the train home and to my horror that I had failed to tell *Newsweek* about the Beatles' Christmas presents or *Time* about the Beatles' Bach.

I was very annoyed with myself because I didn't like failing in my responsibilities to magazines with the dignity and seriousness of purpose of *Time* and *Newsweek*. My goodness, no!

I asked myself what it must have been like being on the road with Jesus. 'Lay your hands on me, Jesus, lay some bread on me, Jesus. Don't get uptight, Jesus. I just didn't get the breaks.'

The government phoned me next day, asking for details of Mr Richard DiLello, an American national 'desirous of seeking employment with the Apple Corps, and requesting a permit allowing him to remain and work in the United Kingdom'. After such an opening, I contemplated the prospect of the remainder of the conversation with much melancholy. 'Mr DiLello', said the government, 'appeared to have no qualifications different from those of an average Englishman.' I said that one qualification Mr DiLello had that was different from an average Englishman, was that he was an average American. The government couldn't see how that could be relevant and I said it was relevant in that the job Mr DiLello was seeking – the one we had – was one that only an American could do. The government at that moment were not unimpressed and there was a pause but then the government said they would need more than that and I, discovering within myself a surprise package of lies, explained that I was a middle-aged square, with a mortgage and children and that as I didn't understand the young American record market and Mr DiLello was in fact the embodiment, a one-man Gallup Poll, of the young emancipated American, he would be able, uniquely, to reflect the best means whereby Apple could tap the American import demand and earn untold and sorely needed dollars for Great Britain. Great Britain.

Richard, his hair like a huge hedgehog, grinned across the room; he had never dared to hope he could stand at such an international crossroads, stand alone, with so many hopes, with the prosperity of the kingdom resting on his dusty buckskin.

Their minds blown, the government thanked me for my

help and many victories were claimed that night and shattered two weeks later when I was again called upon by the government, this time to be asked to explain what I said during the earlier conversation. It is easier to face a surprise package of lies than to remember the evidence offered a fortnight ago. I tried again with, 'I'm a middle-aged square with a mortgage, etc.' to be told by the government that – to paraphrase them – they weren't having any of that old shit, don't try and bullshit us.

Somehow I pulled myself out of that quite well, and at any rate Mr Richard DiLello got his work permit; but in the end many of us despised ourselves for the sly and wily, slimy simpering lies we told the government about Richard, for in truth the only reason why he wanted to work for Apple and for Apple wanting Richard is that we dug him and he dug us, for Christ'sake. One day, I thought, someone is going to have the guts to answer 'because', when someone in the seat of power asks, 'why?'

Because, because, because I want to, because I am, because God made you mine, befuckingcause.

Don't ask me why, I prayed that night and every night, praying that one day someone might tell me something instead of asking.

In those days many people never even made the simplest statement of their name, preferring merely to call themselves *Daily Mail* or *Evening Standard,* can you, will you, may we, we can't, what do you mean we can't, how dare you? Ask not what your Apple can do for you, but rather what you can do for your Apple.

131

I took the day off work today because I couldn't face it, couldn't make it, couldn't get shaved or washed or anything. At the office there were too many colliding lunches to cancel or rearrange, too many open-ended promises to unkeep. So I have taken a day off, a full day sciving, or is it skyving? Or is it neither, for I am sitting typing in the oak-panelled bay overlooking the lawn where Dominic is stumbling and staggering. Maybe I am not skyving at all, but it sure feels like it because I am working today only for myself, I am working for self-gratification and I am enjoying it.

I hope nobody at the office will miss me too much today. I hope life will go on. I mean, I know life will go on, but it will not be the same as if I were there. We change the situation by being there. It changes so much when Allen Klein is in town. It is not the same Apple at all when he is there. It is so much heavier, so much more serious, so much more interesting. I think we need him more than we know. He is the man we love to hate and I am not sure we are fair to him.

Klein has sued the *Sunday Times* for libel. It carried a mean petty piece about him: said he was a liar, a self-publicist, said he was involved in tax-evasion charges, said he went to see Mr Morley Richenberg wearing a dirty polo-necked sweater.

Allen Klein doesn't like being called a dirty, lying,

self-aggrandising tax-dodger. He is funny that way. I don't think the *Sunday Times* should have done it, though I confess I have had more pleasure from the *Sunday Times* than I have from Allen Klein, by and large.

So Allen Klein has sued them and no doubt they will apologise. They should.*

Allen has a scheme which will help the Beatles to recover their lost riches. It will mean that they will have to spend a large portion of the riches they still have, but Allen assures them that everything will be fantastic and so they must be patient.

It must be difficult being patient, waiting to be taken to the cleaners yet again. The fumes, those dry-cleaning fumes again. Jesus, will it ever end? John has an island in Ireland, a country home in Ascot and eighty-five acres and a lake and God knows what else. Paul has a sheep farm in Scotland and a town house in London. Ringo and George have estates in Surrey and between them they have more cars than they or their families could use, yet as often as not the four poor bastards spend their days and evenings in the city talking about gold among some of the smoothest public-school thieves in the universe.

I feel Klein is enjoying himself. He doesn't know everything, but he knows a lot about money and he enjoys it. It is fun to him, it is good clean fun. He knows a buck from a dime; if they were buried in cement, if they were the last currency on earth, he would smell them out. His wife says he is extraordinary. I agree.

His skill, his love, his life, is in dealing. But Mister Bigs like Klein need Mister Smalls upon their backs to bite them,

* And they did.

133

and Mister Bigs need Mr Mammoths at their fronts to smite them. I think Klein is cruel, but I think I quite like him and I think he likes me though neither of us have the slightest idea what drives the other. We are both less than frank, face to face. Maybe we are scared. I know *I* am.

Dick James of Northern Songs came in the other day. Dick was the publisher who met Brian Epstein at the very beginning and did a deal for the Lennon and McCartney songs. He was a small publisher who became very rich and influential because of the success of the Beatles and there is no doubt he behaved very honestly and very properly and also he showed that he was a good publisher, in the sense that he worked the copyrights in what he would call 'the boys' best interests'. He used to say he had a big book and he could tell you exactly what was happening with each song, and he could show that dozens of, hundreds of, thousands of people had recorded the songs and made 'the boys' a whole lot of money.

What has upset 'the boys' is that Dick James has not yet found himself able to meet their needs. They have had meetings with him, short, long, nice, nasty dialogues, trying to show him why it is they believe that 'boys' who write songs should receive more than the 'men' who sell them, but there has been no reason offered that they could accept as a reasonable reason. If Dick could only have said to them, they say, 'because I am better than you are, boys', they might have been able to accept it, in the same way that they have expected him to accept that they should receive more because they are 'better than you are, Dick'. But no dice, no dice 'Dick'; no dice 'boys'. Deadlockery.

And when Dick James came in the other day it was on a very difficult errand. It was to explain to Neil Aspinall why he had sold his own shares and those of his partner to Mr Lew Grade without the knowledge of 'the boys'. Lew Grade? We had all wondered when he would enter our lives like the Demon King in green.

Dick said he would have liked very much to have told John and Paul of his decision to sell his shares to Lew's company, Associated Television, but as they were away, he couldn't risk blowing his cover by passing the information through third parties. He explained that it was a delicate matter and secrecy was terribly important.

George and I were in the room when Dick came in and Neil was sitting by his fire looking sad and lonely and it looked as if it was going to be a fascinating Applechat and heavy as hell, so I asked if we could sit in.

Neil said we were welcome to as long as we didn't interrupt or become facetious or hostile or get in the way. Such promises are easily given, impossible to keep so we gave them and didn't keep them.

Dick James told Neil that he had sold the shares to make his company safer, to protect the future against predators. God, so many warnings against predators. Who the hell are they? We ourselves were warned about predators who are warned about us and we warn about others who warn each other about others so that in the end there is no one we can trust.

George asked Dick if there was no chance of John and Paul making the grade without the help of Lew Grade, for Christ's sake?

Dick said the question was not realistic. The future of Northern Songs had nothing to do with the fantastic talents of John and Paul, in the admiration of whom, he said, he was second to none and there is no doubt he meant it and still does because he is a decent guy and all . . .

'No,' said Dick. 'Northern Songs' future has to do with money and strength.'

I told Dick I thought he was playing with words and Dick appeared not to like this suggestion and he said he had not come to see me, nor had he come to see George, much as he admired George, but he had come to see *Neil*, he said, to explain why Lew Grade appeared to be on the way to owning the words, the music, the art of John Lennon and Paul McCartney (in the admiration of whom Lew had been second to most people, although when gold-dust began to sprinkle their moptops he had, typically, not been unquick to spot it and now he was reaching out his hand to touch the gold for himself).

George told Dick that the trouble was Dick didn't really believe in John and Paul. Dick said that was a cruel, wicked thing to say and I said the truth sometimes sounded cruel and wicked, which was a very righteous and pompous thing to say, but said it was and Dick said: 'When your opinion is needed I will ask for it. I have come here to talk to Neil about private business concerning something very serious to me.'

'Fucking serious to John and Paul,' said George.

Dick never liked rows with Beatles and I cannot blame him. He turned to Neil and said: 'The boys have come under the influence of some very bad advisors recently and I am not talking about you, Neil.'

I guess we all wondered what this dark hint meant. Was it

Klein or was it those 'predators' again or was it really us, the Apple clique with our crazy attitude towards business, the let-it-be-it'll-be-OK amateurs.

George and I left and I regretted being rude as I always do and resolved to apologise to Dick James.

In the London *Daily Mirror* next morning the City editor, Robert Head, wrote: 'Dick James was wrong to sell,' and I felt a little better, but not much. I liked Dick James. He had been there from the early days and surely he couldn't be the enemy. But then, these days, everyone feels like 'the enemy'.

Mr Lew Grade's bid of £9 million for a company built on the talents of John and Paul indicated that the Beatles were a very potent investment, and for all the City's back-street dialogue in the gripping drama ('The Beatles may be silly boys from Liverpool, but they're not without talent'), it was clear that there were sound economic reasons for grubbing around the Fabfour's feet for the remainder of the spring and maybe into the summer if there were still any pennies left lying around. It would be a foolish financier who took an early holiday when there were diamonds still to be mined in Savile Row.

Allen Klein told the Beatles that far from allowing Lew Grade to buy Northern Songs, they themselves should buy the company and not to ask him where the money would come from. It would come, that was easy. He would find it himself if necessary. It was only a few million lousy pounds. Shit, what was that? Allen said it would have been good to buy NEMS, Brian Epstein's old management company who also had a big piece of the Beatles, but too bad, it was now going to Morley Richenberg of Triumph Investment, a 'gentleman' who had refused any more to meet Klein, a 'non-gentleman'. Had it not been Morley Richenberg who had told the *Sunday Times* that Allen Klein had worn a dirty polo neck sweater the last time Klein had been to see him?

It had been a very ugly confrontation. The Beatles were wondering all the time, wondering how they had come to this point where what they had themselves founded, energised, furnished, made in their own image; had turned into a wasteland, a minefield? NEMS, Brian's North End Music Stores, a little provincial company, quite a nice little provincial company, had become, on the backs of the bold bright boy Beatles, a million-pound theatrical agency in Mayfair, now owned by a shiny-shoed city gent who didn't know Aretha Franklin from Archie Andrews.

And as for the government, the government who had forced the hand of NEMS to sell to Richenberg for cash to pay the duties occasioned by the very inconvenient death of Brian Epstein whose money had been well and honourably earned – and at what a *cost*, God rest him – and on which he had paid so much tax already – the government were the biggest tip-off of all. What was the sense in anything? Why stay in England at all, the Beatles were wondering? Jesus, would it never end? How to get out of England, wondered John, whose US visa had been withdrawn because of his bust.

It was strange, we all thought, that America should feel threatened by John Lennon. Big, strong, America frightened of a man because a dry, long-forgotten piece of hashish had been found in his house. Silly, silly. Still, John said, it was no good wondering why because the reality was that America had removed his visa. 'Reality', mused John, 'leaves a lot to the imagination.'

Last night a few friends came round and we Appled for hours, Appling being the inexhaustible pastime of putting our house to rights in theory without having the power to do it in practice. It is like playing Monopoly, and like Monopoly, it can be played by anyone, and often is. Apple staff don't enjoy playing it with non-Applers, however; they ask too many questions and they talk after they have left. God knows to whom, but that they talk is clear from our clippings service.

Last night we concluded that Klein was our best chance of clearing the present muddle, but we wondered if it would create another. Klein is doing what we have all done – drawing up lists of targets and aiming at them but we pride ourselves that we only aim for abstracts – never at people. Maybe that is why we have achieved so little. Klein aims at people – I wonder whom he'll hit?

He says there are some people at Apple who are not helping. Some will have to go, he says. They are not good for the Beatles. He is sure *he* is.

Klein was particularly anxious to 'do something about' Ronald Kass, the American who came to us early to run Apple Records. I am very fond of Ron Kass. His is much that Klein is not. He is handsome, tall and fair, very smooth and courteous and popular. An old friend of mine came to Apple a few weeks ago, came to assemble the Plastic Ono Band, the perspex prototype he built to John and Yoko's specifications to house gadgetry that would play music, screen television, make a light show and all that. Klein and George came into the room while it was being assembled by my friend, Charlie Melling, and they began to Apple.

Klein said Ron Kass would have to go – he was in his way.

139

George wasn't sure. I asked Klein not to remove Kass. I said he wasn't in the way of the rest of us. Klein said: 'Maybe I won't get rid of him. Maybe we give him another job but he will have to take less money.' A fine thing for Ron Kass, take a drop in salary and wash the toilets out. Dubček? Charlie Melling said it was like a movie. He was astounded.

Klein says Ron wasn't necessary? I say that with him we have sold sixteen million records. Klein says that is not the point.

A few days later Klein asks me what's happening, which is his normal opening. I say does he want lunch and he says he does.

So we went to the Santa Lucia restaurant in Rupert Street in Soho, Klein and me and Neil, and while we are lunching we see Germaine Greer, which is beside the point except for name-dropping. She is sitting in the seat Enoch Powell used some time later, but again, that is beside the point but it is all quite curious because the Santa Lucia is a nice restaurant but not fashionable.

At lunch Klein tells me there is some firing going on back at Savile Row. 'A few people are getting hurt,' he says. He explained that he didn't want to be there while it was happening. He said he was having Peter Brown do it because it was better that way. Peter was quite good at firing people – he had a way of coping with it and as these were not his decisions, he could remain detached.

Oh? So who was being fired?

Well, Ron Kass for one.

So.

And a few smaller people, neither here nor there.

Oh.

(Small people were not as important as big people, we once again concluded. It was not nearly so serious for them. They did not have as far to fall. They didn't feel it as much. Small people are something like blacks, their threshold of pain is different. As Henry Cooper says: 'If I had round Negroid features, I wouldn't cut so bad.')

Klein told Neil and me that things could be much worse. Some heads had to roll, that was clear to him. 'You better know it,' he said. 'It could be much worse. Usually I come in and fire everybody.'

Such nice people we are mixing with these days. Fire or be fired. Some choice. The Apple of our dreams was in a hell of a state.

Paul has never been sure about Klein. There was a waiting period during which he toyed with the notion that Klein might, despite his crude thrusts at power, benefit Apple in that he could cut through the clutter of Jobs for Best Friends, Court Favouritisms and all the other handicaps that had arisen from the acid dreams of 1967 when we were all going to live in a Yellow Submarine, when all thy friends would truly be aboard. After this period, Paul decided he didn't like the feel of Klein at all and he called in Lee Eastman, who, like Klein, was a New Yorker but never likely to wear a polo neck sweater clean or dirty when visiting the likes of Morley Richenberg. In short, a gentleman.

Lee Eastman is the father of Linda Eastman. He is a powerful man in New York music publishing circles and neither he nor his son, John, a lawyer, have any love for Klein. So now it was John for Klein, Paul for Eastman. Seconds out of the ring. Klein and Eastman lurched at each other, collided and fell in a heap. John and Paul each claimed victory for their fighters. George, who saw his peace of mind dependent more and more on remaining neutral, said that in his view both had lost.

Klein said: 'Boy, did I show Eastman.' Lee Eastman is believed to have said something similar, though he would no doubt have put it differently, more elegantly.

Outside the ring, the seconds preserved their friendship, but John was still for Klein; Paul still for Eastman, more than ever. John said it was fantastic stuff. It was real theatre. 'It is a pain in the arse having to go to sleep at night,' he said. 'I can't wait for the day to begin again. All these people fighting it out.'

Darker figures were entering our lives. The men in black from the City with fine manners and discreetly leaked statements to the financial press. Northern Songs, said the City, in the person of Ormerod, would not be bid for by the Beatles. This statement I was given for release to the press and it was amazing because it was completely opposite to Klein's stated promise, but maybe in these strange days, that was to be expected. I had the statement typed. It was Friday morning. I asked Neil what the background was, why were the Beatles letting it all go without a fight? Was Lew Grade then to own 'Yesterday' and 'Norwegian Wood' and so on, just like that? Neil said it might not be the final word and by Friday afternoon it wasn't.

Ormerod said a second statement had been prepared. The first was cancelled. The second statement said the Beatles *were* to bid for Northern Songs. I thought it was as well I had not released the first statement. It certainly seemed that the more people talked, the greater the confusion.

As I say, it was Friday when the Beatles bid nine millions for Northern Songs. It was Friday that the big and small men who had been fired left too. One of them went out and got drunk. Not very drunk, just quite drunk. I met him in the lift. His name was Alistair Taylor and he had been with the Beatles boy and man from the beginnings in Liverpool when Epstein had found them. Alistair Taylor's was the signature as witness on the contract they first signed. He had worked in the NEMS record shop, he had been General Manager at NEMS in London, and he was mad about the boys.

A fussy man, Alistair, a 'straight' if you like, but loyal and devoted to the Beatle ethic if there is such a thing. In the lift I said I was sorry about you-know-what.

Alistair said it was OK. 'It's show-business, isn't it?' he said and he introduced us to a silly bald man, twenty years older than anyone else in the lift. 'This', he said, 'is Robin,' and he touched a rose in Robin's lapel. 'Robin is my new friend and he has just become engaged to a very charming young lady. We have both been celebrating.'

Alistair led Robin out of the lift and into the office in which he had served the Beatles for so long, to serve a last short drink to Robin who had just become engaged and that was the end of that. I hope Alistair and Robin and the lady are all right.

Oh dear, oh dear, I think to myself. Oh dear. It is so strange that it has all come to this. We had not foreseen it, Neil, Alistair, Peter, or me, none of us, and yet maybe there had been a little grain of fear back there in 1968 when it was all new because then, at the beginning, I was asked to write an article for *Disc and Music Echo* and I decided to write a piece as if it were twenty years on, as if it were 1988, and all over and changed. The piece was never published. It was too obscure, said *Disc*. Why write about contemporary events as if they were twenty years out of date?

I offer it now, for it might just as well be 1988 for all that remains of the days I described then:

A YEAR FOR NOSTALGIA

It was good then, good when we were young then when we were new and The Apple was fresh and the other apples, wrinkling and shrivelling in creaking barrels tended by old misers and ghostly villeins, drew their shroud-skins more tightly around themselves and said, 'They'll learn, they'll learn it's no fun, no fun at all.'

It was though. It was fun in Wigmore Street with the office-Beatles, hobbits entranced by their new spring business-suits sprinkled with bright buttons, mandalas and daisies which winked reassurance at the other young revolutionaries and seemed to say: 'We're still on your side, don't let the suits deceive you.'

In the early shining summer of 1968 we had Apple Music, Apple Shops, Apple Films and Apple Electronics and we hadn't made a record and we hadn't made a film. We hadn't sold a single invention and we hadn't opened any shops outside London and what is more we had spent nearly a million pounds of the Beatles' money. So it was then, when 'But surely it's time you had a record out', 'But don't you think it's time . . .', 'But it can't be possible for the Beatles . . .';

when most of the questions began like that we said 'Yes' or 'No' or 'Wait' because even then it was beyond doubt, beyond the far shaded tip of a shadow of doubt within any of us forty or so at Apple, that in the fullness of time, the hits would mount and the albums increase across the universe so that every village which had passed the Age of Mud would have the green Apple apple smiling at them from the record stand beside the player, beyond doubt that the patents of the inventions of Magic Alex Mardas were safe from the thievery of the business bandits who at the beginning of time would have stolen the blue-print for childbirth had they been Abel. One week the *Observer* came to Apple to see, the *Mirror* to reflect, and both were drolly surprised to find that John and Paul came in daily and on time, whatever the time, which, for Paul was about half past ten and for John, a man of erratic sleep, three hours later. Each stayed until nightfall and further in those days and my goodness we kept busy. We had suggestion boxes for suggestions and the amazing thing was that the suggestions were read and interpreted and, incredibly, implemented in many cases. 'I suggest we . . .' Done. 'May we please have . . .?' Certainly.

A time-and-motion man would have lost his reason in those days in Wigmore Street. I had a slim shoebox of a room and such were our promises of a hearing for anyone with something creative to offer, anyone off the street who was frustrated with years of screaming for someone to listen, any singer who could climb a scale, anyone with a piece of coloured paper which he called a painting, any caller with rhyme he believed to be poetry, any Fellini of the 1970s, such was our published pledge to be a market place for the lowly artist, a gathering of Beautiful People, that by dusk any night there could be a duo of guitarists 'better than Clapton'; a

Mancunian who saw himself as a mingling of 'Mr Kite', 'John Wesley Harding', 'Billy Shears', 'The Mighty Quinn' and 'Popeye the Sailor Man' and having thus seen himself, sought £50,000 to make a film of him acting out the fantasy; a Californian author-to-be with hair like a hedge in Heswell; a sculptress who had never sculpted but who wanted facilities to make a nude out of patent leather and then cover it in oil to induce 'tactile delight' (you and whose army?); a Geordie who had caught the Parisian inflections of his French girl-friend and who wanted a flat in which to rehearse – and me, sitting on the floor, on the windowsill, in the waste paper basket, on our hands, on each other's head, all this and cups of tea and cigarettes and Scotch and ahead, a train to dark Dorking, all this in a cupboard tolerable only to a typist cowed by years of pain.

But it was good because we met some fine people and some terrible people and that's how it goes. In the big corner room, John and Paul and George and Ringo would play host to those with goods to sell and needs to be met. Nilsson came there after arriving in England and met Kenny Everett there and Twiggy came the day before with Justin, her boy-friend, both of them looking wonderful and happy, and quite rightly. Ron Kass, Apple Music head, fresh to Apple in 1968 from the chieftancy of the outriding Liberty Records International Division, walking with diplomacy from room to room, learning the strange dialect of the Liverpudlian and there were lots of us then – and the Beatles, they were from there, too.

Well, they said in the Town, the Town outside our world in Wigmore Street, 'It's just an old pals' club.' 'Well, Town,' we said, 'it is. Old pals and new pals and business with pleasure and also a profit and you know it can't be bad.'

Yes, but what did we *do* then, in 1968 when we had only

two signed singers. Two? Yes. James Taylor, sharp-eyed, made of bone and wire in North Carolina, and Mary Hopkin, fashioned in dew, freckled and shy and mini in a mini skirt from the Rhondda Valley. What tasks had we, when the third Beatles' film had neither name nor script, nor contract, when Apple Publishing looked for its first hit?

Well what we did was we planned and talked and laughed and got ready for when – for whenever. We each found work to do and from each other we took work and to each other we gave work and thus we found the very work we liked doing and the very work we did best and we did it well and some of us thought it would have been wonderful always to have been allowed to carve our jobs out of a stone of our own choosing rather than have choked all those years on the dust of the chalk thrown to us in the name of WORK as a four-lettered euphemism for slavery.

16 / About 1969 – written 1969.
Bad, black day at Montagu Square

It was a very good morning and the advertising man had been and gone. The advertising man was more than forty and less than middle-aged but the years were telling and there was the faint red and purple sheen of the boozer who had shaved well and slept badly.

The advertising man had come because the night before Paul had said we should get something very good going for the new album, 'You know, really make a scene out of it because it is a great album: made a new man of me just listening to it.'

Thirty tracks on the new albums and it had taken five months, only. What a long, long haul from May to October, but we got plenty time for the waiting game. *Variety* had become confused and said that the new Beatles album would feature John Lennon and Yoko Ono nude and would be called *Yellow Submarine*. Who was to blame them except a few words with someone would have got it right for them. The press is full of good eavesdroppers and bad listeners.

Well, so much for the good morning and the advertising man. At about noon Neil came into the room and said, 'Could I have a word with you?'

He said he had just phoned John and it looked as if John had been busted. He said he had phoned John at the flat and a strange voice had answered the phone. 'One of those voices. One of THEM,' said Neil and the voice had said John was not there.

'Who are you?' the voice had said, and Neil had replied, 'Never mind, I want John.' 'Who are *you*?' the voice asked again, with no name of its own. Who behaves like that, who but the law of the land? Come along with me.

'Who are *you*, who are *you*?'

Neil said, 'Neil Aspinall,' hoping he had nothing to fear, and the voice said John was occupied and couldn't speak. Neil heard John muttering in the background, and then after a silence, John's voice said into the phone: 'Tell Derek to cancel that press conference today.' Neil said, 'OK, but why?'

John had replied. 'Imagine your worst paranoia, because it's here.'

That was what Neil told me and he said it seemed as if John had been busted.

Busted? BUSTED!

Two American girls had come in; they said they worked with a disc jockey whom I knew in Hogsville. One girl was dark and one was fair. The dark one was Katy and she was chewing gum, rolling it out, now and again, pink and gnarled, on the tip of her tongue. They were mannerly and conditioned in the American way, working to a unified script, that had been not memorised, but rather dyed into their conversation. 'You must be Mr Taylor; gee this place is really neat. Quite a building to work in; you must be very happy working here. I hope we're not interrupting anything.' 'No. Have a glass of champagne.' 'Wow, thanks. I wish I worked here. Really neat. Thanks.'

I gave the fair one, Laurie, a copy of George's album *Wonderwall* and the conversation inexplicably took a curve into the elections: 'I think I'll vote for Nixon,' said Laurie. 'He seems safer.'

Safer?

I went downstairs for a copy of the Beatles biography by H. Davies of Malta. Neil was settling down talking to someone about something which had nothing to do with busts. It looked as if it may have been a false alarm after all. I got a biography, signed 'John, Paul, George, etc.' and took it upstairs to hand to Laurie who said this was their lucky day, really neat.

Katy looked very down. I found a second copy of *Wonderwall* and gave it to her. She brightened up and I said, 'The book is for both of you, by the way. You'll have to share it.' Laurie's grip on it tightened, and she hugged it to her and said, 'Wow. I've got it. It's mine.'

I took it back and wrote on the inside, 'To Katy and Laurie,' and Katy would have hugged me if she'd been five and mine, but at twenty it was too late for innocent hugs if you come from Hogsville.

Ronan O'Rahilly, Pirate King of the Sixties, told of the mystery of John (by Jeremy Banks who'd been whispered to by me), phoned Neil and offered any help he could give. Neil came upstairs, and took Jeremy outside the room and left the door open. We heard the beginnings of one of the 'whydidyoutellhim,' 'I thought he oughttoknow', 'Youhadnoright', 'Ihadeveryright', discussions that punctuate the day in corporations large, and corps small, so I closed the door so we couldn't hear any more. I hate earwigging rows.

Then Neil asked me to go down, and while he was repeating much the same thing to me, the phone rang. 'It's Peter Brown,' said Barbara, the secretary with the mostest secrets.

It *had* been a bust.

'Where are you?' said Neil down the phone.

'At John's.'

'The police there?'

'Yes, more later, must go.'

Action Stations, OK.

I phoned Joan and asked how was she, because John had been busted. 'Oh, poor man,' she said, 'poor fellow, the bastards do that.' She said, 'What a day.' Cohn-Bendit had been refused an entry permit to stand for the Rectorship of Edinburgh University. 'The bastards,' said Joan. 'The fuckin' swine,' said I, and we had a couple of minutes like that and then we said a warm good-bye and Ray Connolly phoned.

'John's been arrested,' he said. The *Evening Standard* are very quick on tip-offs. They appear to know things simultaneously with Caxton Hall, Scotland Yard, the Royal Docks, the London Clinic, Guys, the Krays, you name it, the *Standard* has it. Many pieces of silver change hands between Beaverbrook Newspapers and the fawn raincoats who whisper second-hand secrets down the public phone.

Ray is a good man, and very straight. 'He is a fool, isn't he,' he said. 'I said it would happen.'

Jeremy said the phones were probably bugged. 'I have feedback which says they're tapping the lines,' he muttered. So I told Ray in a voice which was obviously unnaturally loud, and therefore more unconvincing than ever, 'We never take drugs, Ray. It is most improper of you to say so, ON THE

151

TELEPHONE. How DARE YOU LIBEL us?' 'Cops,' said Ray, 'I'm very sorry.' Don Short was on the other line; 'It's happened,' he said. I said I knew.

Don was sympathetic, then he laughed; 'Trouble is, I've got a couple of other dodgy stories for tomorrow. One is that John's dad has married. The other is that Yoko's pregnant.'

'Thanks, Don, thanks man.'

'Can you confirm?'

'No, Don. Not at the moment. Can we leave it over? Till Monday?'

'Yes, better, much better,' he said. 'I mean drugs, adultery and his father. It's a bit much, all in one day, even for the leader of the Beatles.'

Don too is a good man who must be rescued from Fleet Street, or who better still, must save himself.

It started to feel as if it were lunchtime or maybe later, but in the circumstances we didn't feel like eating and in the circumstances we didn't feel we should smoke anything and in the circumstances even Jeremy's offer of prescribed Librium appeared unsafe, so we did what we'd always done, what we used to do all the time in the old days. We drank.

Jeremy had Scotch and I had brandy; ice came from upstairs. The phones were buzzing pretty hard by now. Michael Housego from the *Sketch* called and said, 'I suppose you've heard.'

'Suppose so, Michael.'

'Not much you can say is there, Derek?'

'No, Michael, there isn't,' I wished I could see his face, find out if he were smiling – I was glad I couldn't see his face. He was certain to be smiling. They were all certain to be

152

smiling. Do the press ever weep? Well, it was, in newspaper terms, a good story. No doubt about it. It was what some of them call a biggie. A very biggie. The *Evening Standard* called again. Ray said, 'They're at the station now. They've been charged with obstruction.' Well now.

That would mean they hadn't wanted the police to come in the house. Does anyone want the police in their house, ever? I suppose if you'd been burgled you would want the police in your house. I dare say you would. I hope I'm never burgled. I don't ever want the police in my house, especially two of them at once. There's always one of the two who doesn't smile. You see him at all the police gigs. He's the one who looks you up and down, from the top of your louse-ridden head, down past the dark immorality of your private parts to the tip of your improper shoes, and then he looks you up and down, again and again, and he does not smile.

Even as a child he didn't smile.

Tony Barrow phoned. He said, 'Hello mate.' Mate? 'Hello mate,' he said. 'Keep me posted.'

Woman's Own phones. It was Maggie Peters wanting to know which famous people, apart from Twiggy and Paul McCartney, Mary Hopkin had met since she came to London. I said we were a little busy with a domestic problem and would she please talk to Jack Oliver about the famous people – apart from Paul McCartney and Twiggy, whom Mary Hopkin had met since she came to London – and I was glad later that I hadn't said, 'As if it fucking matters, Maggie, which famous people any of us ever meet,' because it crossed my mind that our world must seem very strange to come-up-the-hard-way journalists like Maggie Peters, confronted as they now are, in the pursuit of stories of pop musicians, with pictures of scrotums, tales of cocaine, cannabis, heroin, lysergic acid, methedrine, abortions and idols who refuse to marry. It's a long way from the days of Doris. It is far away, and thank God for that I think but I am too conditioned to know for sure. Maybe I want to be a traditionalist but I am too disturbed to allow myself to stay where it's safe and old.

Dorothy Bacon from *Life* called. She wanted immediately one final picture of Mary to complete the cover story. She hadn't heard the news of John either, and one wondered whether sometimes the immediate media – TV, the evening papers – didn't overestimate their power, for there are in truth many people out and about in the thick of city life, who have no idea what is going on around them.

I phoned Mary at the Caprice restaurant and she gave me a medium but not rare hard time about the picture for *Life* because, as she explained, 'I'm with my mother, so I don't want my picture taken.' It took a couple of minutes to persuade her, and not for the first time I was glad to be under pressure, because a minor issue becomes easy to accomplish. However nice Mary's mother, her needs seemed very small fry compared to the dilemma of John and Yoko.

Bob Barr of Westinghouse phoned and, with the smoothness of the better American journalists, asked for some quick background. I told him what had happened and how it could come about and what could overtake even a Beatle with the MBE, and much of his adult life devoted to the making of music, the spreading of fun and fantasy when, having pulled up his roots and fled his home, he had finally

154

and completely forfeited the protection of the Establishment by posing naked with a woman not his wife for the cover of his own record album.

Ringo was in Sardinia and I phoned him, clear as a bell, and softened the conversation's opening by telling him the album was finished, 'All thirty tracks, Ringo.' 'I know,' he said without puzzlement, though he must have wondered why one phoned at noon on a Friday when he was on holiday to tell him something he must have known for the last twenty-four hours. Neil brought a proper sense of direction to the conversation by taking the phone and saying: 'Hi Ring; Neil here. I've got bad news . . .' Neil is very blunt.

We couldn't trace George in Los Angeles, and we couldn't work out why, until much later that night when we discovered that Zsa Zsa Gabor had not been able to vacate her home in time for George's arrival as temporary tenant, and that as a result, his agents in LA had placed him, in the meantime, in what must be the only dwelling place in all of that electronic city not to have a telephone.

Newsweek, *The People*, *Women's Wear Daily* and a German disc jockey had to be phoned and asked not to turn up to discuss John's record album with him. 'For obvious reasons,' we said with some archness. Some archness, but not enough for *The People* whose Peter Oakes, with extraordinary single-mindedness, pursued his needs to the point of asking, 'Do you know when John will be able to get together with us?'

'Aunt Mimi', said Peter Brown, 'was in tears.'

What sort of boy had she brought up? How had she gone wrong with John? Wrong? Four photographers in raincoats, stone-faced, irritable, sour, tense, arrived at Savile Row in search of John and Paul. 'Can we be blunt?' asked one. Certainly. 'We need pictures,' he said. Amazing.

Paul returned, chatty and cheerful and sort of shaved. Inwardly he must have felt terrible and not only inwardly was this shown. He ruffled his hair endlessly and cracked the sort of jokes with which the best uncles seek to soften the horrors of the worst funerals.

Ivan Vaughan was with him, the Ivan who had introduced him at fourteen to John, drunk at sixteen, at a Saturday afternoon garden fete in Liverpool, many centuries earlier. Peter Shotton arrived, Pete from Quarrybank School, never far from John's side in emergencies in the sixties. Tom Wilkes from A&M Records in Hollywood rang and said he'd heard about it on the LA radio. It was not, he said, unexpected. No it wasn't. When, we all wondered, would they come for us? I dare say some of us wished it could be soon; let's get it over.

I phoned the *New Musical Express* to sound them out for an ad we might put in, raising a 'legalise freedom' petition. Percy Dickens said he didn't know. The same paper had earlier turned down the picture of two naked backsides. What's worse, hashish or a bare arse? Both probably; or neither.

The evening papers arrived. 'Lennon and Yoko' was the main story. Not John any more. 'Lennon.' A fan called, tearfully, for news and said, 'God bless you.' Mick Jagger was phoned and told on the set of his movie. He offered advice and love. Brian Jones called and sympathised. Now we're truly all one and the Beatles were as *persona non* Scotland Yard *grata* as the Stones. And the thought for one and all was who has the right to say it must be John who fronts for our drug-smoking? Should we all present ourselves at the police station and surrender? We may have thought we should on Friday, but I notice none of us actually did it. Cowards or Men of Discretion? I don't know. Cowards, would be more likely, I think. Lazy and cowardly.

They lost. They paid.

We all won. We don't go to jail no more. No small thanks to them.

17 / About 1969 – written immediately. More about the jolly British bobby

It is not nice knocking at your own front door and having it answered by someone you have never seen before.

But it is most particularly a bad scene if the person you have never seen before is a cop you have never seen before.

It is most particularly of all not nice to knock at your own front door and have it answered by a cop who tells you he is busting you for possession of a dangerous drug or two or more dangerous drugs. Just how many will be decided by the police analysts. Just how dangerous dangerous drugs are has not yet been decided by anyone, but that is another story. For sure, no one ever died of smoking a joint. Any suppressed government report will tell you that.

This now is a story of a young man and his wife having eight cops and a lady cop and two dog cops as guests all of a sudden on the evening of the day the young man's friend and colleague – no less than Paul McCartney – got married in front of the world. This is the last day you would want to give coffee to cops.

George Harrison heard over the phone he'd been busted from Pattie who was in the house when Sergeant Career Cop – 'I have a duty to protect and serve the community' – had arrived to sniff around and ferret in their personal belongings, with seven other bluff bobbies, plus a lady and a couple of silly Labradors in a severe state of withdrawal.

It was just a routine visit, the sort of thing that could happen to the Beatles any day, any time of the day, any time of the night, but better than ever in C. Cop's – necessarily limited – view to bust George on Paul's wedding day. Confronted with so much youthful happiness, what would anyone do? Add to the happiness, or take away from it? What would *you* do to make more memorable a guy's wedding day? You would arrest one of his best friends, wouldn't you? Admit it. You wouldn't? Then you'd never make a cop.

The law was right next to Pattie, said Pattie, as she phoned George. I was with George in Apple when they spoke. George thought maybe it would be better for Pattie to show the law 'the stuff', just lead him straight to it, or maybe not.

She didn't in the end, but the dog found it anyway. Found more than George and Pattie thought they had. That's not unusual. What would it be like if eight cops and a lady cop entered a Beatle's home and found nothing? That wouldn't look too good. As it happened, there was no need to plant, the stuff was already there.

In Savile Row, Peter Brown phoned Release, looking for the reliable Martin Polden, the civil solicitor who, because of some loop of destiny now found himself the most prized pot lawyer East of Manhattan and amazed to be that way, most amazed and probably, though he never showed it, sometimes a little nervous. Civil liberties lawyers are not liked by the establishment.

Martin was away but one of his colleagues was there. George phoned friend Pete Shotton who also lived in Esher, said we were waiting for the lawyer, would Pete call on Pattie, make out he was just dropping in casually, sit with her,

159

dilute the cop-content, bring some friendly vibes. 'Of course, of course,' said Pete, and left for George's house immediately. The lawyer arrived at Savile Row, a bit nervous at meeting a Beatle and George said he was for telling the cops to fuck off, he was anxious to own up proudly to pot as one of the more (though small) agreeable features in his life.

The lawyer said that wouldn't help. George said it was the truth and the lawyer, who was not a bad man, became even more nervous. The *truth*? Great heavens, let's leave the truth out of it for a moment, we're talking about the Law. You mean the Law has not to do with the truth? The Law has to do with what is lawful and what is unlawful.

I understand; let's leave the truth out of it for the moment. Quite. It was not long before we had left the truth out of it so completely that the three of us were tap-dancing around the extraordinarily untruthful proposition that George should deny smoking pot, knowing anything about the filthy rotten mind-eroding devilweed.

That, in the event, a plea of guilty was entered was due not only to George's concession to his conscience, but also to the reality of the coffee table in the living room at the Esher house which was in truth and verily, verily a social pot-smoker's dream. Hashish from the Lebanon and King-dom of Nepal, marijuana from Mexico and papers from the noble Captain Rizla, papers orange, papers green. Pipes too, from San Francisco and Asia and the Holy Land, and joss sticks of many scents and secrets.

We arrived in Esher and knocked at the door.

'Come in,' the cop said generously, and many solemn men in several rooms rose and put on their silly soft felt hats and gathered their height to its fullness and spread their shoulders to their extent and bounced upon their boots with robust anticipation. Hold that moment, catch that dream. West End Central has got themselves their second Beatle. Arise Inspector Decency.

The record player was playing a new Beatle album unreleased, unmixed as yet. The television was on, half on, but on and the bobby in the small trilby ordered: 'Turn those down,' and then he charged George and said he had charged Patricia Ann Harrison, as she was referred to, who meantime, was pouring wine in the kitchen, watched by a police lady in her thirties who had put on a new pair of tights for her special evening out in Esher.

George drank his wine and looked at the men in the hats and said, 'What are all these men with hats on doing in my house? Badgers have holes and birds have nests but man hath nowhere to lay his head.' The men appeared not to understand. Pilchard said it was time to leave and said that as the bail bondsman I should follow in another car. I thought that would be fine and saw the first party to the car. A weasel in a raincoat ran to the front door and exploded a flash bulb in our faces. This, apparently, had something to do with the freedom of the press but it appeared to have very little to do with the liberty of the individual, or with a citizen's right to privacy on his own good soil, or with commonest courtesies or with simple dignity.

Do you know what goes into the making of your morning paper? It is much the same as what goes into the making of your morning bacon. A lot of flesh gets ripped off. Have you seen the little piggies . . .?

161

The old cops left a young cop to watch me. I supposed that it was more of a drag for them than for the young cop, for the young cop was there from choice. Can you imagine that? From *choice*? The cops said it was a warm evening, I said it was, and in no time at all – God knows why – the two of us were discussing men who expose themselves indecently on tow-paths.

The cop said it probably had something to do with the abolition of capital punishment? Yes? I said I had just read *In Cold Blood* and the young cop became considerably freaked as I told of Perry Smith and his friend and the many wicked murders and the hanging and the rottenness of it all. The cop was quite amazed.

Later, in the car to the station, the sardonic old cops escorting me asked me where Peter Brown was. Big joke. Peter Brown, always bailer of the Beatles. Big fucking in-joke, if only to a handful of cops, but in enough for it to be offered to me, but now the grass that had carried me through the night did a double somersault and left me emotionally sprawled on the floor. It was a terrible evening. George was fined £250 and Pattie was fined £250 and some of the nice righteous right-wing newspapers commented on the leniency of the fine: 'Not nearly enough.'

Lenient? It was the maximum. It was the *maximum* fine. Lenient? Fuck off, it was lenient. Bring back the cat, the birch, the lash, the gallows. Punish, punish, punish.

Good luck.

I am a lazy cunt yet I never worked harder than last year, and I never worked less.

It was not a difficult year and nothing literary got saved, nothing. It was a great waste of time by day and very valuable by night, at home. Joan and I and the kids really got to know and love each other and found why we had come back to boring old England, complacent and grey and petty though it is, we found out why we had come back.

The point about last year, a terrible year at Apple, fluid and open but terrible, is that there was nothing you could blame. There was no fad or fancy, no whim, trend or fantasy to follow or hold close. It was a nothing year in the history books to come, a nothing year anywhere except America and the New Nixon, for there it was, the end of the beginning and the beginning of the end, and if you have read that before it is because it has applied before. Phil Ochs had to be spat at and Mailer arrested, Joan Baez and her mother had to be gaoled, Chicago had to happen and the nation ripped open before *Life* magazine was ready to tell us that: 'If it should turn out that the enemy does not want peace, a carefully phased moderate troop withdrawal would give the US plenty of leeway for second thoughts in case of Communist bad faith – and is a far wiser way of smoking out Hanoi's

163

intentions than a new round of potentially self-fulfilling threats of escalation.'

As you will agree.

John Lennon was on the *Eamonn Andrews Show* the other night with Yoko. There were people on the show and at the show who wondered what the hell John and Yoko thought they were doing in bed and who the hell they thought they were to do it and why the hell should any normal person put up with it and when would it stop and where would it lead us and how would it bring peace to the world (bearing in mind that there has never been any and that there never will be, for haven't all the fat and weary intellectuals told us that 'All You Need Is Love' is banal, trite and oversimplified. 'I mean I've smoked pot like these Beatles but that was years ago in Oxford when it wasn't fashionable and anyway it made me sick so give me the old bottle of rosé and a good row anyday.') They say that it was just a piece of profiteering Beatle nonsense, and what the hell is beautiful about acorns for peace?

Yoko and John were sending two acorns to world leaders so that they would plant them and grow oak trees for peace. 'What's so good about acorns?' the man in the audience still wanted to know and John said again that oaks grew from them. 'Do you like trees?' he asked and the man didn't reply. 'Don't you like trees?' asked John. The man said, 'Yes, I like trees, but that isn't the point, what have acorns to do with trees?' John said that acorns had a lot to do with trees. The man waved such nonsense aside and the studio audience, seduced from an evening of viewing by the promise of being viewed with Eamonn, applauded the common sense of the man who was Anti-Acorn, possibly the first time this particular minority cause had received public recognition and, indeed, approbation.

Jack Benny was on the show with John and Yoko and there was one very fine dramatic moment when he stood up and said, 'I wouldn't get involved in this row for a million dollars,' all of this with that famous clasping of his hands which, in their splendid theatricality, almost, but only almost and not really, obscured Benny's real commitment which ran, right down the line faithfully from Bob Hope, hopeless in his emigrant-patriot paranoia, solid with the forces of Light Freedom and Truth against the Red Hordes, wheeling in from the East in Chariots of flaming shit. Still, Jack Benny is Jack Benny.

John said he didn't worry about communism, later told a friend he would have said, better red than dead, but he had to think of the Beatles' image! Communists, yet?

Yehudi Menuhin who is also there, pointed out that there were certain circumstances in which it was necessary to kill. John wondered what these circumstances might be. He wondered to himself if Yehudi Menuhin would be prepared to be killed right then and there if, as a result, world peace could be reached. He asked Yehudi if Jesus [who?] had said anything about certain circumstances when it was necessary to kill. Yehudi says that is not the point. John says, 'What did Jesus say? Did he say anything about killing?' Yehudi coughs and says, 'No, Jesus didn't but he didn't say anything about staying in bed at the Hilton in Amsterdam.' It is then John's cue to say that nowhere in the New Testament (nor, for that matter, in the Old) is there anything about violins, but he doesn't say this because already the audience are applauding Yehudi Menuhin, the violinist, for his wit.

It was a dumb daft nothing-solved evening on *The Eamonn Andrews Show* and it was not helped by the presence of a Rolf Harris who didn't want no boats rocked either.

John and Yoko, Jack Benny, Yehudi Menuhin, Rolf Harris, Eamonn Andrews! Was it all a dream?

No it wasn't, yes it was. It happened but it happened *in* a dream and though we were all awake we couldn't remember much so we were treating it as a dream which is why the serious grownups thought we were daft.

Me, I think the grownups are daft. They are Martians, sitting on the trains with their erections hidden under their *Evening Standards*. I hate them. Try and sell them acorns . . .

19 / About 1970 – written 1970.
Upyer, all of yer

There are about eighty things wrong with working for the Beatles and one of them is that there aren't any Beatles any more and another is that one forgets who one is, whoever one may be; the experience of working for the Beatles has affected all of us in different ways, but affected us it has and forever; come what may we will never be the same.

Simon Albury of BBC 24 Hours told me yesterday that when he was making a film of John for the BBC, he became increasingly frightened by the growing awareness that John's only concern was for Yoko and for no one else. I realised, he said, that if John heard that everyone at Apple had been killed in a fire, his mind would turn immediately to the inconvenience of replacing them. He said that this feeling was the more bizarre because John was such a kind man, very courteous and thoughtful in little ways and so he is and so too would he not give two pennies if everyone on earth vanished into the oceans leaving himself and Yoko in peace, however imperfect.

Aunt Mimi taught him his manners well and there is in all of that family, whom I met, a gracefulness that has passed to John, but sentimental he isn't, never; neither is Paul and I don't think George and Ringo are, but is anyone really *that* concerned about anyone else, I mean *really* worried about their fellow humans? I don't mean Shelter and Oxfam and

Bangladesh, but what about the rest? John himself and George, and Paul and Ringo too, in differing ways, have given away stacks of money to causes good and unproven, always given it quietly. But they are very tough, too, and working for them has made all of us very uneasy – I think because they are four very hard tight men, not callous, but calloused. Us Beatles' aides, we come and go and we are mostly unmourned when we have gone.

For myself, I have no complaints.

I came because I wanted to and I left because I wanted to and I came back because I wanted to and because George wanted me to and I have stayed with George because we both wanted it, but I am still uneasy because I still have the utmost difficulty remembering to remind myself that I am because I am, I think therefore I am, I am therefore I think. I think so anyway, but I am not always sure.

You know, it is a pain in the arse going out and being introduced as Derek Taylor of the Beatles. If I can get away with it, I can say 'I make plastic toys, that is my trade', but they want to know what sort of plastic toys and so on. Or I can say I am a writer and they will say what have you written and I should say I write about 2,000 words a day about the Beatles or associated subjects and then I am back as Beatles' aide again.

Derek Taylor, ex-press officer of the ex-Beatles is my new role, and this is even less satisfactory if you are seeking a sense of self in order to be. 'I'd like to introduce myself; I am Derek Taylor and I used to be the Beatles' press officer when they were Beatles.' What is that? I get the horrors thinking about the year 2000 when *Late Night Line-Up* send for me to talk about the good old days when the Beatles were kings. It is the sort of thing Wee Georgie Wood is dragged out of his snail-shell to perform for George Robey and the other dead heads of music hall. We few, we happy few who swung with the Beatles, we are stranded now with our heads full of knowledge about a subject which has been dropped from the curriculum only to reappear on the twenty-fifth anniversary of the release of 'Love Me Do'. We are experts in something which no longer exists. We are Monty's batmen wandering through the desert, stumbling over buried tanks; where have all the battles gone? Where once we were contemporary (was there ever anything more contemporary than the Beatles?) we are now keepers of archives, and still too young to play historian to vanished moptops. So what did you do in the war, Daddy? Kept me end up, son, kept smiling when all seemed lost.

Oh, it has been a great adventure, and we all shared the fun. The Beatles were generous with the fun. The Beatles liked the people around them and the people around them liked the Beatles.

We were not sycophants, yet we were rarely bold. I think we were always nervous because there were four of them, and only four. There were two assets common to those who survived a close relationship with them: 1. We didn't want to be Beatles and we didn't ever think about their money; 2. We were good at what we did and what we did *they* couldn't do.

But it wasn't always enough, I felt, because in the final analysis, they were themselves enough and any of the aides could go jump off the Empire State Building and the show could go on, but if any one of them had a sore throat, the rasping could be heard from Newcastle-under-Lyme to Singapore. I was a very good press officer for them, and there was no doubt about that and I could reflect some of their best interests and speak their truth, but the quotes were theirs and there is no comparison between a mouth and a mouthpiece.

In other words, the question 'Who am I?' is not easily answered by a press officer/agent/director/publicist, but it is a question you have to keep on asking. Oh yes, it is OK to be known as good at it ('He's very hip and intelligent, he's from the same town as they are'), but it isn't really enough and I think the second time around as their press officer, I only took the mouthpiece out of the role-closet and strapped it under my moustache because it didn't really fit anyone else. I didn't want it, but if the cap fits . . . don't worry about whether you enjoy wearing it.

I don't know whether to laugh or cry now that it's over. I mean I *miss* the Beatles, they were part of all our lives and all our loving, and yet it is nice for them and for us from the inner clique to be ourselves, so again, I ask, who are we? Will we ever be allowed to go out and about as normals, or will we always be offered bones to inspect and label: 'Which one was it who really split them up?' 'Who was your favourite?'

I dunno, I dunno, I think sometimes that the people closest to them are the people the Beatles resent most. We were so adjacent to the truth, to the money, so near to the fame, and the success and all of the glamglitscreamcheer that we got to look very like courtiers, covered in gold dust. Did they ever think: 'Goddamn them! Who do they think they are? Who needs them? *We* are the Beatles, we are the four.'

To press and public we had many faces. We were the link,

the pipeline, the barrier, the obstacle course to be cleared to reach the big prize, but it was just a job, y'know, you know how that riff runs.

Neil and Mal and me and Peter, we were there because we wanted to serve the Beatles, we were heavy fans, so are all the people around them; I guess the whole world is and the miracle is not that the Beatles survived the world's adoration (they didn't, they took a powder to end the pain), but that Lennon and McCartney and Harrison and Starkey had the wit and the wisdom to cling to the good earth and not fall off.

Clinging to reality can take a lot out of a man and I think that towards the end, they were looking at us like parents having troubles enough of their own, looking at a houseful of full-grown sons, sitting around making tea. If any of them had said, 'Why don't you lot go out and get a job?' was the feeling I got, so here I am, sitting at this desk.

When I was with the Beach Boys, says the old soldier, recalling past glories, the Beach Boys and I were talking about how we all lived off each other and one of them said: 'We couldn't make it alone,' and I said how come we managed before we met. Mike Love said: 'Listen, we ate then and we'll eat when it's over, it's irrelevant.'

So it is but like I say, if you live in the foothills, you don't like rumbling noises in the night, it makes you paranoic.

I don't know what was worse, being with the Beatles when hellish pressures sent us screaming into the arms of the wicked pill doctors or being with them when everything was cool. You know, some days my tongue was thick and red and swollen and sore, with talking and explaining, setting the record straight with so many incredibly stupid

171

mediamen, women and children, yet those were the good days when you could have died with your boots on, man, like a hero. But now that it is quiet and it is ended, we are very thin-lipped and analytical, quiescent, taciturn and it is hard to see the old days like they were. Did it happen, all of it, or was it a dream? Like, was John once married to a girl from Hoylake, Cheshire? Did George actually sit in the Whisky à Go Go with the other three and Jayne Mansfield (Jayne *Mans*field?) in Hollywood throwing a whisky over Mamie Van Doren or was it coca-cola? You must be joking. None of it ever happened.

So, having come by many loops to this point, I now conclude with the comforting thought that we are all of us, Beatles and aides, moral, temporal and striving to find an answer. I am going to Ascot Races and will see you again, tomorrow.

Ascot was very nice indeed, very. It is the day before the election and Labour are going to win so Ascot is extra nice.

Labour didn't win and we go to a barbecue, Tories on toast and five hours of Herby Alpert and someone saying I suppose this isn't your sort of music. Don't bother to tell him used to work for HA, know him, like him etc., too complex to tell him that.

Also, the man knows I am with the Beatles and he is telling me that pop music is 'fixed', in that kids are bribed by record companies to go around buying up a single so that it will be in the Hit Parade (*sic*, sick) ha, ha, ha. He says a man in a very (*very*) senior position with EMI told him all the tricks.

I say, oh no, pop music is a very clean industry, no one's

going to be fooled into buying anything they don't like. He asks, 'What is it that sells a record then? Sheer talent?' Warning buzzer sounds in Beatles Sensory Cell, he is going to put the boot in any minute. 'No, not necessarily sheer talent, it is the sound that sells, the sound.' That sounds trite, but it is true, it is true, it is the only way to put it.

He is not impressed. He says, 'The kids will buy anything that is in the hit parade.' Oh no, oh no. The kids will not buy anything they don't like. A record is only in the hit parade (there I go, now I'm using it: *hit parade* – indeed) because the kids have bought it, that is how it gets into the hit parade. He says the hit parade is fixed. I say who fixes it, the BBC? He smiles knowingly, he rubs together his thumb and second finger, and says, 'Kids, bribed by record companies.' I say kids aren't corrupt, not like grownups. He says, 'I remain unconvinced. I am square.' I say of course he is square and he has a closed mind.

Oh no he hasn't, he says, far from it. Then the boot. For the third time I hear the phrase 'sheer talent'. 'So, it's sheer talent, is it?' he is saying. He smiles. 'ARE YOU TRYING TO TELL ME THE BEATLES HAVE ANY TALENT?' he climaxes. Here it is, it is the old, old story. I say to Joan: 'Isn't this when we take a walk?' She smiles and says, 'Yes.' We walk. He is very cross because it has never happened to him before. In *his* game, you don't walk; you stay and discuss, politely, or impolitely, you make your point. You argue, debate.

Not us, man, not us. It wasn't good for the barbecue, I think. He must have told his wife because she gave us the bird too, later. Why do we ever go out except among our own, why?

More . . .

Another guy asks me what on earth John Lennon is doing with that house (a Georgian place a mile down the road from where we are barbecuing each other) and I say I don't know, but he isn't living in it. He says it is a pity John isn't living in it, what with it being such a fine house. I say, 'It's a fine house,' and he gets very excited and says: 'Oh you agree do you? Well I'm very glad to hear that.'

I figure he is very uptight about John having the house at all and that he is going to become rude about J and Y, so somehow we drop the subject. A lady says she would like to know the truth about J and Y and I say I don't know the truth, does anyone, and the lady asks is it true they had been so badly burned by local contractors that in despair and disgust they had fled to America? I said it was unlikely they would fly 7,000 miles to escape the bad vibes of contractors who would always and everywhere be screwing the Beatles.

The lady said wasn't it silly of people to burn a Beatle. 'After all, no one is ever going to re-employ a contractor who has burned him.' I said the contractors shared the squares' view that as the Beatles were only a flash in the pan, you could do what you like to them, but quick, charge them as much as possible, but don't delay.

I don't know what's worse, moving among people who don't know them or mixing with people who do. The topic remains the same, Beatles, Beatles, Beatles. It's only the approach to the topic that varies.

I have an acquaintance in Canada who came to visit me on tour and said he wanted to see me and talk about old times, he didn't want to bother the Beatles, not him; but by evening he had hired a photographer, hidden him in the backstage area at Maple Leaf Stadium so that he could get a quick snapshot of himself with the fabs, 'For my kids, Derek, not for myself. Believe me, forgive me.'

Sure, sure. It's not for me to forgive you, E. It's for you to forgive yourself.

20 / About 1967, year of acid – written in 1970. Monday, another Monday

Another of those days, another Monday, half over already and nothing to show for it except I weeded the little Alpine garden under the new pear trees and moved the rabbits round by the side of the sunroom and then made the sunroom like it wanted to be sat in, instead of skirted because it was so tatty and full of nothing. I sat and talked to my father about old times and new, and we had beer. He has retired now, for the second time, and he seems to have changed levels. When he was sixty-five, he retired for the first time and he sat at home doing crosswords and dying. But now, at eighty, he has taken up painting and has joined an art class and a club (Conservative, but he may be forgiven) and he's moved to the seaside and I must say it gives me great encouragement for myself in AD 2012. On Saturday I said we were going out boozing, was he coming? Certainly, he said, rising from the sofa to prepare himself, in a sand-coloured suit from Nutters in Savile Row. Later, he got quite pissed and I played him some old 78s. We all went off to bed happy.

This morning I planted fourteen shoots of Wandering Jew, *Tradescantia*, a plant easily tended and propagated indoors; there are about a hundred around the house now, grown from a single shoot picked up for half a crown somewhere sometime when there were half-crowns. Like I say, it's another of those days, another Monday, half over already and nothing to show for it, nothing on the typewriter, anyway. Joan said every time she comes in a door, any door, she finds me sulking and fiddling, anything to keep away from writing. I said maybe it would be more interesting to become the man with the greatest collection of Wandering Jews in the country or maybe, even, in the world. She said that was all very well, but on my deathbed I may well regret squandering a life on such an easily tended and easily propagated plant.

She is probably right, yet it is marvellous to work with something as responsive as a plant which is not only living, but thriving and reproducing faster than the fastest rabbit.

Well, OK, enough about the Wandering Jew, but I'm sure you'll agree it is a pretty plant.

I lost you halfway through that sentence. I picked up a copy of *Record Retailer* and there was a picture of the Sandpipers who were the squarest group in the world when I last saw them, boy were they STRAIGHT.

I met them in 1965 when Tommy LiPuma from A&M (he is now with Blue Thumb, hi Tommy!) asked me would I write a biography on them (bio in the trade), because he had produced an album based on the runaway hit 'Guantanemera' which he'd pinched from a Pete Seeger album, pinched in the nicest way because Pete would get royalties on it and anything Pete Seeger can get, he deserves. Pete had pinched it from a faraway revolution, the hero of which would have been glad to know his song had fared so well.

The Sandpipers were quite a dull bunch of ex-Mitchell Boy Choristers by which I don't mean to be rude, but by which I am, so I withdraw the word 'dull' and substitute the word 'boring' which again is a bit harsh for three kids who never harmed anyone, so maybe the word is 'uninteresting'. I don't know. What I mean to say is that *I* didn't find them interesting, and maybe they didn't find me interesting. I wrote the bio, though, and I wrote a liner note.

I was pleased with the liner note and also with the $125 that A&M paid me, not only because I needed it but because it gave me, for the first time, a price I could charge for myself. The liner itself was a before-breakfast trip, about twenty minutes, but two years later when I met up with A&M to try and find a price for working a day a week (purely hack work; weneedalinernoteintenmins, OKyougotit, whoisitaboutnot-thatitmatters), they asked me what I would expect to be paid so I said about $125 a day, like that liner note I did, please.

The Sandpipers came to me privately that year (1967) and said they would like a day of my time to discuss their image, or rather their manager did. They said: 'How much?' and I said, 'What about $125 a day like that liner note.' They said, or rather their manager did, OK, and he brought one of them to my office which was part of the Monterey Festival set-up on Sunset Boulevard (opposite Gene Autrey's 'Continental Hotel' with its 'no longhairs' rule, and the sheriff's men come by for coffee every morning, in khaki, leathers and gunbelts and steel helmets, which was *really* nice) one morning in June.

The Sandpipers talked to me for four hours and I became very tired and irritable because although they wanted to roughen their image, they didn't want to change their attitude, their appearance or their music which kinda made it tough for me to advise them.

It really came down, in the end, to each of us saying 'What can I tell ya?' which never leads you anywhere. I said why don't you wear scarves instead of ties and grow some hair on your head and, even, on your faces and finally they left grumpily nodding that they would, but they didn't. Not until now, when I notice, three years later they have done it because it was that or die and I'm not claiming I had anything to do with it; I didn't, but if they'd done it *then* they would have been early for once instead of late as usual.

I also advised them to take some acid but from the look of their scarves and the look in their eyes as I look at them now, it's clear they didn't. Anyway, it didn't really matter what fee we fixed, did it, because after four hours of talking about scarves and moustaches no one had the heart to exchange money and I have written the time off to experience.

It was an idyll, was 1967, the year of *Sgt Pepper* and acid and drugs of many colours. Monterey Pop Festival, of which more somewhere else, and A&M and the Byrds and other people all paid us enough to live on and no one overworked that year except maybe the Sandpipers and Paul Revere who was never one to relax when there was money to be picked off the Yucca trees. At A&M we launched a massive campaign by mail and, next, the public. One of the poems I wrote for the mailer read like this: grattig snalsog shoghot binging harold schwein . . .

And so on.

George was given his visa back; the US Government had revoked it after he had pleaded guilty to possessing the dreaded and deadly cannabis resin which causes euphoria and introspection and God knows what else. Now he had it back again, valid for three weeks, but he mustn't engage in gainful employment while in the US, nor attempt to over-throw the government nor indulge in prostitution. Pattie and Terry Doran agreed.

So we caught a jumbo to New York, and this is what hap-pened as far as I can remember. At Heathrow a girl from the airline said she would take us upstairs to the private club where we could have a few drinks before take-off. She apol-ogised for the climb and we said it was quite all right. She asked were we economy or first class and we said we were travelling first class, but as for *being* first class, that was a matter for debate. She said all she was getting at was that if we were first class we would have more time for drink-ing. That was nice for me to hear but George was indifferent. He doesn't drink a lot and today he had a bag of Krishna beads made and presented by Shyam Sundar-Das, one of the London Krishna temple who was presently engaged on car-pentry work at Friar Park, George's Gothic revival pile at Henley-on-Thames in Oxfordshire where another Krishna devotee Deva Data (from Westmoreland) was putting the thirty-acre garden straight (the *Daily Mirror* having pointed out that it had been neglected for twenty years. Jealousy will get you nowhere, *Daily Mirror*).

What with chanting the maha mantra, Hare Krishna, Hare Krishna, Krishna, Krishna, Hare Hare Hare Rama Hare Rama Rama Rama Hare Hare and counting the beads, there wasn't going to be much call for whisky on this flight, thought George. In the club, Pattie had coffee, and George did and Terry and I had whisky and coca-cola, an unusual drink commented the waiter, so unusual that practically everyone we know has been drinking it since 1963.

We left the club and Pattie kissed George good-bye. She kissed me good-bye and said do look after him and I hoped I could. I hoped he could look after me too. I hoped we could look after each other. I wondered who would look after any of us if the plane should dive into one of the gravel pits in Staines.

We went through immigration, outwards and walked through the tunnel and into the jumbo. One of the hostesses shrieked: 'A famous person, I've got a famous person on my flight.' We sat down and put on our safety belts, and the girl came over and said it was him, wasn't it, it was him? George said no it wasn't and the girl said it had to be. She said she had never had anyone famous on her flight, well that wasn't true, she had had Gregory Peck but his wife had been so hostile. She hoped we wouldn't be hostile. She was very excited by it all and George said she might be better to cool it, as it was a long flight and we weren't yet off the ground. He put his hand in his blue Krishna bag and began to chant under his breath. The hostess went back to welcome other passengers who were not famous. A steward came on board. He looked like Omar Sharif and we thought he probably smoked pot.

The plane took off and to my amazement it didn't crash over Staines; the faces of the other passengers began to assume characteristics. There was the pale man and the red-faced man and the old lady with grandchildren and the spinster and the man who had flown a lot and the starer who would just have to make an approach before Kennedy Airport. For the time being, he just stared. Later he became a grinner, hanging back and grinning and staring. There is usually a staring grinner when there is a Beatle around.

Before lunch, someone said that if we wanted to get high after we had eaten, there was a joint available. No thanks, man. Jesus! What it is to have a conviction for smoking. You might just as well carry the words 'dope fiend' on your forehead ever after. There was much fussing and bowing and some very pleasant attentive service throughout the flight, due almost entirely, so far as we could see, to George's fame and due partly to the minimal demands we made on the crew. We are not difficult passengers, we were saying to ourselves, and it was true enough. The girl who had welcomed a 'famous person' finally hit George for autographs and she said: 'You have been no trouble at all.' 'Neither have you,' we said.

The grinner made his approach an hour before Kennedy. He was in the travel business, he said, and here was his card if we should ever tire of the high life. He said it was OK being him, he said, because he was a nobody, but it was tough living where he did because of the MARIJUANA PROBLEM. There

182

it was again: were we just wealthy symbols of the drug sub-culture, so that anyone who had ever smoked felt they had to approach us as fellow conspirators. We supposed we were. Well, OK. But don't give us any more grass, man. Don't forget we only just got George's visa back after eighteen months. Don't get us busted at Kennedy, for Christ's sake.

We landed safely and said good-bye to the crew. Our names were called in immigration and an official said Pete Bennett was there. Pete is Allen Klein's promotion man and fixer. He is very stocky is Pete, with a deep suntan and you can betcha he has a lot of black hair on his chest and shoulders and back. He chews a cigar and he is short and he has fancy linings in his suits and a label that says custom tailored for Pete Bennett. He is about forty and he can fix most things; also he is very nice and to important people he is very kind and generous. He would be kind and generous to unimportant people, if he ever met any. But he doesn't any more. Who is important and who is unimportant? Don't ask me. Ask Pete Bennett. The people he has been photographed with are really important. Such as Lindsay and Nixon and Elvis and George and Senator Goodell and so on. Maybe the most important of them all is Peter Bennett.

We sailed through immigration and customs in three minutes flat, our path smoothed by Pete's fix. UPI and AP met us on the freedom side of the barrier. 'No pictures,' cried Pete, putting an arm round George's shoulder and grinning into the lens. 'Absolutely no pictures.' We limousined into Manhattan and even felt glad to be there.

It was warm as can be in New York and humid. I was glad I'd brought no coat. George had his hair in an elastic

183

band and he had stopped chanting by the time we reached mid-Manhattan. There was so much to see. Pete said he had got Ringo's album a lot of airplay and likewise Paul's and he would work his ass off for George when his album was complete. George saw the New York Krishna devotees dancing and chanting on Sixth Avenue and it felt like home. At the apartment, on 53rd and 7th, Allen Klein joined us and Paul, Klein's runner, showed us a full refrigerator and a willing smile. Paul was another good fixer: tutored by Pete he would become a great one.

It was evening by now and we didn't think we would go out. We switched on the television and it was worse than we remembered it. Such noise. Such commerce. Such colour. Nixon was to decide, with his advisors, whether to invade Cambodia and it was very heavy. Off with TV. Allen Klein told us he was releasing 'Long and Winding Road' as a single and George wondered what the Beatles would think. Allen's father had died and we were very sorry. George's parents weren't well either and my father is, as you now know, eighty, so we were able to relate to Allen more than he suspected. Allen left, likewise Pete and Paul, and George told Al Aronowitz from the *New York Post* what had gone down in the past twelve months while I made a huge meal of scrambled eggs (twelve) and three vegetables, spinach, corn and green beans, for which they both thanked me. Neither of them enjoyed the meal, nor did I. We threw it away and it hasn't been mentioned until now. I will never forget it. It was beautifully cooked, but it looked terrible. It was just too much.

By ten o'clock I was falling asleep sitting up so I went to bed. George and Al talked some more and then Al split.

Next day we woke very early. Me at five, George at seven. We had tea and breakfast and by mid-morning we were on the street, with Al, buying shades, and then I tried to get a travellers' cheque cashed in the Underwriters Trust Bank. A bouncer bade us good-day and frisked us with his eyes. The cheque was refused: 'The amount it is too big sir,' said the girl. On Broadway we saw a gang of Klein's people leaving for his father's funeral. They said they would cash the cheque and in the meantime George lent me $120 and we went off to Miller's and then to Kauffman's to buy western things, denims and so on. I phoned Joan from the booth in the store and across the ocean we communicated about chest measurements and what size shoes did Vanessa wear. Easier than phoning Berkshire from Harrods, and really it was lovely to be back in America where so much of life is easier if you don't care about politics, which we do, only not when we are buying denims and cowboy hats, not then. At Kauffman's the owner said he was in showbiz once, 'I'm a lawyer,' he said. He showed me a Xerox of a cartoon from the *New Yorker* which said: 'Why don't we get out of Cambodia and stay in Vietnam where we belong.' I pocketed the Xerox and I still have it to this day.

We were about 250 bucks lighter by now and feeling good and so we went to Hudson's, a very tough store which sells any amount of cheap tat and some good stuff too. The populace looked pretty hungry and evil, so I watched the car while Al and George shopped around. George tried to ask for boots and the clerk said unless he had got the exact catalogue

185

number he could go fuck himself. George took over watching the car and I bought four baseball hats, three pairs of white cotton socks, about six dollars in all, and asked for a basketball out the window. 'No,' said the man, 'I'm not getting it out the window. You can buy a basketball any place in town.' It was $3.95, the basketball. (I bought one later, in Abercrombie and Fitch, just before closing time on Saturday. It was $18.50. No less. You will shop cheaply at Hudson's, if they let you. You will spend a fortune at Abercrombie and Fitch's and they will always let you.) A hippie bouncing a tennis ball came by and said: 'Boy is this town uptight. I'm from San Francisco. I'm going to Spain to groove, man. This town is so uptight.' A black woman with a shaved head told a wasp with a face like a lemon: 'Just stay out of this, wench. Mind your own.'

Then we went to Manny's. Manny's is the big musical instrument shop in New York. They have signed pictures of anyone who ever played or sang a note for public acclaim and they asked me could I get new ones of the guys, signed. Yes. George borrowed a new phased guitar, Gibson, and an amp and was prevailed to try out new equipment. A small and nice crowd gathered. I leaned against another wall and a hippie said it was groovy to see George, really groovy, what instrument did John play on 'Mother Nature's Son'. Stokely Carmichael was in the store with Miriam Makeba. Manny introduced George, Stokely was pretty distant. Miriam Makeba smiled. Well, well.

Al said it would be good to unload the goods at the apartment and drive to Central Park.

Central Park wasn't looking good. Poor squirrels to be born

and bred and beaten down in Central Park. One squirmed across our path, resting every couple of feet to catch what was left of his breath, a few wheezes and a little choking sound, its legs all over the place and its poor tail a shabby wisp, a dead bush. There was a zoo nearby, hot and nasty and we baulked at the first cage and left, buying the US flag on a stick for fifty cents. 'Vote for Rao' for Congress, said the lamp-posts. Rao looked out at us, fleshy and narrow eyed with the thin, frustrated mouth and clamped jaw of the American Dream unrealised. Al drove us through mid-town Manhattan in his new car. It was very big and dusty and quite new. It broke down fifteen minutes after he took delivery, he said. Then a front window had been forced and his stereo deck ripped out. Nothing surprising in that, he said. His little boys had been mugged and robbed more times than they could remember, just walking back from school. Once, maybe twice, it had happened in the elevator of their apartment block. Suffer the little children, and the big children. Four days later four were to be murdered at Kent State University and one of the National Guardsmen would say: 'It was like we were told to clean out a latrine. You do what you were told.' The same puppetmasters who can't stop Al's kids being mugged on their doorstep can have students slaughtered on campus. There *is* a conspiracy; there are nearly 200 million people involved in it. The aim is suicide.[*]

We had lunch at the Brasserie. It is French in a way and American in a way and the combination is very nice. We went back to the apartment and George phoned Bob Dylan who said come round tomorrow. Tomorrow we did go round

[*] I went again to New York after all, twice in 1972. It has changed. It has decided to live. Good, good, good.

to where he lives in the village, but first we had a few words with our sponsor, Allen Klein, who was quite benign and very businesslike. I said it was good he wasn't a pretty man. If he was, he would never get up. He sure has to suffer a lot of abuse. Did he ever kill anyone? Murderers have had more kind things said about them than Allen has. He needs friends. He can have me for one if he wants. I don't hate him.

Before we went to see Klein in his terrifying offices on Broadway, we entertained a member of the Press; just one. It was Howard Smith who works for WABC FM Radio and the *Village Voice.* He is OK. He has a moustache and a lot to say which is just as well if you earn your living broadcasting and writing. He got just about the best interview George ever gave. It is interesting these days sitting in on one of these solo interviews, wondering how the web would have been woven if all four had been together again, answering the same questions. No wonder God, the Devil, Popes and Premiers weren't discussed in the old days. The wit got in the way of the wisdom. But it doesn't matter. To everything there is a season and if you valued the Beatles and believed their influence to be ennobling (and if you don't, what are you doing reading this?), then it was well they were witty and flippant at a time when they were winning the millions.

At Dylan's that night we heard his new album and I met him properly for the first time. He is a very decent man, father of five and he looks as if he doesn't overdo anything. He played some tunes on the piano, some new and some old, and asked George would he do some recording with him next day. We drank some cognac and some coffee and met a painter friend from Woodstock, a big cheerful man called Something or Other, with a pretty wife with a face that looked very serious, anxious even, in repose. Who can tell about people, who can tell?

At midnight, Al and I left for a short walk round the village. We had a whisky or two in somewhere and met Ramblin' Jack in the street. We took George home and we all went to bed.

That was in the spring of 1970 and it is now 1972, near enough two full years later; silly to say a lot has changed. What for instance? The album Bob Dylan had played us was named *Self Portrait* and it was not well reviewed but we played it at home last night. 'Blue Moon' and 'Let It Be Me' and 'The Mighty Quinn', and maybe I like too many things, maybe I have no critical faculty but it sure sounded good. Later Dylan made *New Morning* and that was well reviewed and they all said he had found himself again and it is so sad and so awful that people keep undiscovering and rediscovering these artists who are doing the best they can when they can, as they can, and sometimes it doesn't come off. Too bad, too sad, sod it. It is quite all right you know, there is a lot of fun around. So what else happened?

To Allen Klein for instance? He got sued by Mick Jagger and the Stones and he sued James Taylor. He was alleged to have ripped off Bangladesh's starving millions so he sued *New York Magazine* for $150 million and (pardon me *New York Magazine*) if *New York Magazine* has a spare 150 pennies to pay a libel suit then I should be very surprised. Albert G. tells me one of Allen's lawyers left ABKCO's employ recently and there were at that time 146 lawsuits pending which must be some sort of record or some sort of exaggeration and either

189

way, I pass it on because figures like 146 pending lawsuits or libel actions for $150 million have always impressed me. Klein didn't rip off Bangladesh. No fear. He is not evil. He does his best to be good.

I met Allen Klein in the street in London recently and he grabbed me in a bear hug and danced around saying, 'How ya bin,' and things like that and also, 'I always ask for you, betcha I ask after you more than you ask afta me.' 'True, Allen,' I said, 'but there are times when it is easy to love you, like now I love you, Allen.'

He is a funny one and no mistake. No doubt about that. Three corners of that old Beatle block still have plenty of faith in him and they have all made some nice records since he took the weight of the money off their backs on to his. In the years between my end of Apple and now I saw nothing of Paul but the other day I had a phone call, right on the lunch-hour, a favourite time for him to call, especially out of the blue or out of the brown or whatever room or study he was in and it would always depend on what had just happened to him which colour he would be – same for all of us I guess – and we talked for an hour about Life Itself and Music and Klein and it was nice to hear from him and I hope we can make it through the rest of our lives, just having nice conversations about this and that without getting uptight. But I don't care to discuss money or Klein with him and I don't care for all Paul's views on other things. Many other things happened.

I have been working for Warner Reprise for a year and a half now. They gave me a nice title: 'Director of Special Projects'. Very grand and very true.

For a time it was bewildering being with a new group of

people, out of the Beatles' umbrella, working with such a long list of artists, and you can find it confusing doing work for Rod McKuen, Alice Cooper and Frank Sinatra and Fanny in one week, never mind in one minute, and it is as well I have a parenthetic mind. I wrote a movie treatment, a terrifically mediocre potboiler which was anyway quite as good as anything of its type, like for instance I don't suppose *Easy Rider* looked much on quarto sheets . . .

Anyway, my relief was boundless when no one wanted to make the movie which was about a Northern band who made it big, managed by a young bachelor, moved to London, toured America and called themselves the Myce (any resemblance to anyone living or dead is entirely coincidental and I don't have to pay lawsuits of $150 million either) so imagine my horror when Tony Calder, a friend who commissioned the script, said Laurence Harvey adored the work, wanted to direct the film and play the manager.

I went to see Harvey who was playing a schoolmaster in a melodrama at the Queen's Theatre in London and we talked about the work and he thought it was very fine stuff which really brought me down. In those days – this was 1971 and it was still a struggle finding an identity (see 'You Know You're Not Really Any Good You Know') – I had a chilling sensation in my blood when anything to do with Beatles or Myce was mentioned but I shouldn't have worried because Harvey's play was taken off, our planned dinner was cancelled ('I can honestly say this is the very first time I have ever had to cancel anyone out,' says Larry, call me Larry. Oh yeah? The very *first* time? Fish gotta swim, Byrds gotta fly, actors gotta charm'n charm till they die). The script was stolen from his limousine and up to now the Myce haven't left their holes in my brain and if they never do, it will be too soon.

I am really enjoying life you know, thought you'd like to know. This book is my Personal Statement, I guess and I am going to call it Foul Stories of Necrophilia by Derek Taylor, rather than bothering to ask the publishers of the song by Herman Hupfeld for permission to use their words 'As Time Goes By' for the title, although there is much truth in the idea that a kiss is still a kiss, just as there is great truth in the idea that a sigh is just a sigh, and also in the words 'I Want to Hold Your Hand', and this brings me to the way the seventies are turning out. I think they are turning out very badly. But our gang are still treating each other with much tolerance and if we can extend it to those we don't care for, then maybe things will indeed get better, get better all the time.

22 / About the past – written anytime.
Critics and critics and victims

I was wondering how to do away with half-informed critics without harming freedom of speech. Conclude there is no way to accomplish their downfall, conclude also that there is no need to. Best remedy is not to read them. But who are they, the instant critics, and why?

I was a 'critic' once, for the *Daily Express*. My qualifications were that I was a trained newspaperman who knew more about show-business than anyone else on either the *Sunday Express* or the *Daily Express* in Manchester, which was saying very little.

I'd been working for the *Sunday Express* for a couple of years, since the closure of the *Sunday Dispatch*, since the closure of the *News Chronicle*, since the strike at the *Liverpool Daily Post & Echo*, all of which had combined to propel me into Beaverbrook Newspapers whose policies in general were attractive to few of us, but whose status and rewards were appreciably higher than most others in Manchester. Anyway, a job was a job.

For most of the 1960s, both the *Sunday Express* and the *Daily Express* in that city were favoured (if that is the word) with editors who took a friendly view of the entertainment industry. Editors were the ones who got to meet the stars on their best behaviour, at the cocktail parties and banquets and receptions. They had tickets for first nights and even if their duties prevented them from attending many, they felt an affection for the cinema and for the theatre (but not for television which they rarely saw) which was reflected in the space they offered me.

Generous, some said, to a fault was my space and Richard O'Sullivan who covered industry and who was nearly ninety and certainly in the shade, thought it was a crime that anyone who, for singing, earned in a night more than the Managing Director of ICI earned in an afternoon, didn't receive at least fifty strokes of the birch and a red-hot poker up his arse. Anyway, anyway, when I was on holiday in the Isle of Man in the summer of 1962 when Frank Ifield was the big new thing, 'I remember Yoo-hoo' (do *you* remember?), Howard Bygrave, Manchester Editor of the *Sunday Express* phoned me. Urgent, said the hotel, urgent, and I left the beach to take the call, uncertain as to whether my expense claim had finally bounced or whether I was being sued for libel, but certain that it must be one of these two.

Of course, folks, it was neither but just a nice friendly call to say that Arthur Brittenden, editor of the *Daily Express* was thinking of taking me on as showbizman and theatre critic and that he, Bygrave, would not stand in my way. 'Think of the scope,' he said, and I thought of the scope and there's no doubt that it was looking like a very good break. I mean, I really did love show-business and I still do. I think it is absolutely vital for our survival that we have this great well of music and drama and laughter and song to fill our boots, to wash away our pain, to renew our psyche, it doesn't matter whether it's the Beatles or Ibsen or

Gilbert or Sullivan or Pinter or Mahler, but we seem to need something.

But *critics*, where do *they* come in?

I waited some weeks after Bygrave's phone call, panicky weeks, a period of exquisite paranoia, would I or wouldn't I and if not me, then who? And, when you boil it down, one said, how much did one really know about the theatre? Was one learned enough, substantial enough, mature enough? – all those fears. Well, probably one wasn't, probably one wasn't, but one got the job anyway.

First decent-sized piece I had in the *Daily Express* was a feature on Frank Ifield ('with a smile as wide and as white as Sydney Harbour Bridge' – a bridge I had never seen and which, when I did see it, turned out not to be white, and not even to be very wide. Silly stuff, silly journalese), and next to the byline (oh joyous byline, how coveted in those striving days . . . that's ME there, ME in print) was a faggish picture of me smirking in a 'Double Two' shirt. That day I went to Blackpool to interview Nina & Frederick, big, big stars then, and they said they liked the piece on Ifield, so I wrote one on them that I thought they would like, and they did and all of a sudden I was swinging with the narcissism of the business and it was tremendous fun filling space with warm complimentary stuff about people I liked.

However, it was made clear, there had to be conflict ('a little acid,' Bygrave had said) and not so much of the flattery please.

My chance to introduce 'a little acid' came the following Monday when Derek Bond, Jean Kent, Griffith Jones and others who had towered in the forties, collided in a comeback, a play at the Opera House, Manchester. My piece was quite rude, mean even, and it could bring the unhappy cast no joy when they opened their *Daily Express* on Tuesday morning, and though I did the same to other plays over the next two years, and though readers and staff at the *Daily Express* were very pleased with me, I think there were few moments when I wasn't aware that what I was doing had no validity, no humanity, no point, purpose or possible defence except that I was paid to watch plays and write about them and that, in the scheme of things, I had the RIGHT.

On balance, I was much nicer than nasty, but that too became a drag, because the basis of the exercise was suspect. You take a man from here, you sit him there, you bid him watch and listen and then you order him to write, to write up to the edge of libel. It takes, the whole thing, four hours, maybe five. Next day, many, many millions of people are invited to share your judgement and also, depending on one's credibility or readability (and sometimes – maybe always – the two coincide), the public are turned off something *they* might have enjoyed and supported.

Play, producers, backers and cast, time spent creating, time spent in production, loving care and attention, real and earnest endeavour, very often something akin to lifeblood, all these are cast aside in two, three, four hundred words from a sour competitive man driven by who knows what motivation, prejudice or hangup, fighting the clock and sometimes quite pissed as well.

Of course, of course, I know, I know . . . not everyone is into the criticism game because they have a desire to spite or harm (though there are some very shitty people with powerful pens and a great distaste for their milieu, whether it be politics or the theatre), but what I am wondering is why anyone would become a critic, and *stay* one, even, in most cases, to the grave; few critics retire – criticism is too easy and too cosy for retirement to have any fascination.

In my critical boyhood I was no Presley maniac. You'd find me in many a bar falling off my elbow with indignation about this decadent slob who couldn't write his name (the besetting sin of reporters is that they believe what they read in the newspapers and in those days the straight press never wrote anything nice about Elvis), but I was so much older then, I'm younger than that now.

And after him, in the days of the late fifties and early sixties (when, as Harry Nilsson said, every American pop singer was called either Johnny or Bobby), there wasn't much pop I could relate to, but then came the Beatles to the Odeon Cinema, Manchester in May 1963, and I fell. The groundswell of 'mature' criticism of the Beatles was considerable in 1963 (the band's conquest of many squares was only accomplished in 1964 when the American nation fell in love with them) and there were people in senior positions in all newspapers who doubted the permanence of their success. It is to the credit of the editor Arthur Brittenden and then his successor John Buchanan, a much maligned man, that they saw merit in liking the Beatles and through their support I was able to write pages of undiluted praise on behalf of the fabs.

Finally, I joined their staff because beside them, everything else seemed pale and in the years since, as the publicist in me transcended fifteen years of (impartial?) reportage, I have wondered a lot about critics.

197

23 / About the recent past – written 1971.
Believe in the music, it will set you free

Paul once reminded me, 'Don't forget, you're not very good, any of you, you know that, don't you?' I *had* forgotten, I *had*. It had gotten to the point where I was really believing in myself, you know, really having a good time being me.

Apple was in its (comparatively) early days. I had been back from America three months, this was summer 1968. It was design time for stationery and advertisements and logos, we were building our image by being and that was trouble, being. Being was sticking your neck out and getting bites all over it. I don't think I ever hated anyone as much as I hated Paul in the summer of 1968. Postcards would arrive at my house from America or Scotland or wherever, some outright nasty ones, some with no meaning that I could see, one with a postage stamp torn in half and pasted neatly showing the gap between the two halves. Joan received one bearing the words: 'Tell your boy to obey the schoolmasters,' and signed: 'Patron.' Far out.

Lots of people were getting postcards in those days; Christ, you know it wasn't easy. These were the days long before Klein came to town. These were the days when Neil Aspinall as Managing Director would come to my room in Apple in the middle of the day and collapse on the sofa and sit, staring and staring.

He tells me now it was fear.

I knew then it was fear. We were all frightened. We were frightened of Them and we were frightened of each other and we were frightened of the press. At about this time Paul wrote 'Hey Jude'. Remember: make a sad song better.

We are in summer now, 1971, and I work steadily and happily these days for WEA, the conglomerate that bought Warner Reprise, who had bought Atlantic and Elektra and I earn a lot of money (looking after some things and some people), and from time to time I read things about myself in the over and below ground newspapers without which the music business seems unable to believe in its own existence.

Melody Maker, pointing out that apart from me, everyone at WEA was under thirty-five, said I was eloquent and world weary, living in the past. Ritchie Yorke in *Pop*, a new publication offered this week as the alternative alternative newspaper, said I was a celebrity extraordinaire, I was 'honest and frightened of nothing and no one' (I should be so lucky) and he said also that I was a gentleman described by some as brutal. Liner notes on albums say I am 'gentle', my hometown newspaper calls me 'successful', not knowing, how could they, that my happiest working days were spent long ago on that very newspaper, and this week I continue to resist (my modesty having temporarily cooled my scorching desire to communicate) approaches to be interviewed by none other than the *Windsor Express*.

Time Out, heavily ironic, call me 'a pop mighty, remember him? Fifth Beatle?' The *Guardian* says I am 'experienced and pragmatic' and George Melly on BBC Radio reassures his listeners that contrary to the image they may have of the

199

Beatles' publicist being frenetic and trendy, I am actually very decent and intelligent and rather nice.

Now, all of this is of considerable unimportance because it alters nothing that I am, but it is of some interest to me because it begs the whole question of who the hell are any of us to write about the rest of us and I would ask all of you to take all of this with a pinch of rock salt, because it is only a view from a sitting position on a very hot afternoon in Sunningdale, Berkshire or from a standing position in a very hot situation these last years, believe it though, and let it be because it does seem my confidence has returned after three years which is when this book should have been finished – three years ago at least.

Something happened last week which was most significant – I signed my name with a flourish and it was a legible signature and it said: Derek Taylor. In the ordinary way I dare say this would mean very little – but it was fantastic how good it felt at the time. I blame no one but myself and I mention it only because it happened and it was wonderful.

As I said, it was three years ago this month that Paul said to us: 'Remember, you're not really any good, any of you, you know that, don't you?' My God, it had been a long fight uphill most of the way, learning how to be and I credit the Beatles with astonishingly generous support for my efforts.

My job in journalism was going very well indeed when we met, if you regard the Beaverbrook Press as something of value – and I did then, don't now, hate its attitudes and stinking bigotry with fierce passion – then I was making some good time for myself but then I met the Beatles and that was the something else that millions of us were to pick up on and feed off and feed and feed off in one great seven-year feast.

They broadened my vision and narrowed my margins of error, they straightened my path, loosened my tie, and they taught me to stand up and speak out. They hastened my classlessness, turned me on and inside out, literally put acid in my tea and in Joan's, gave me presents, took my word for a lot of things, took my views on other things, my praise when it was offered free, bought my labour when it was offered for money and in the end, and in the end, by December 1970, I suffered an identity loss so crucial that when Richard DiLello returned to the Apple he had joined as an office boy and left as an apathetic wreck, returned as photographer and designer of the last Apple Christmas card which was to feature all our tense, cautious faces, I walked like a robot to a white expensively designed hollow white plastic rhomboid, placed it over my head, sat in the Director's chair and posed faceless as one of the 365 arses Yoko once filmed. It was time to leave, I guess, and I went. It was New Year's Eve 1970.

You have read about the early part of that year, when George had sent me home: 'Write,' he said, 'you have a lot to say.'

Dear George. I have nothing to say about George that isn't loving and warm, and elder brotherly. Considering everything, he is a saint. He sent me home because there was nothing left for me to save at Apple – I don't think I knew the half, not a quarter, not a tiny fraction of the background to staff movements in the last days of Pompeii, when the boiling shit hit the fan and sprayed over leaders and followers alike, leaving us all feeling grubby and ugly and useless.

Was it true then, like Paul had said, and John was later to

say and say and say again, that we were all of us, the inner clique, worthless, talentless?

No, it was not true.

We're alive . . . and to prove it, we're here.

An hour ago I was sitting here and messing about on the desk when I found a clippings envelope, unopened, dated 26 August 1970, and I opened it, and inside was a short piece with a picture of the four of Them and Yoko, from the *Aberdeen Press and Journal,* which read very nicely, if uneventfully, and regretted the passing of the Beatles. One paragraph read: 'The highlight of the film is the finale on the roof with its sad irony, the four swinging into "Get Back",' and another described 'Beatle-starved people who emerged from the surrounding buildings to listen wherever they can find a perch or a stance, snarling up the traffic, bringing the working day to a standstill, baffling the police.'

The article concludes: 'A real happening!'

We all remember that day at Apple because it was so incredibly happy – it was the Beatles live, in the open air and in public, but it was not insignificant that they chose a roof-top, their own private rooftop, out of reach, and for the most part out of view, to do their last show together.

I remembered too that when the film was finally released, almost disowned by its stars, Piccadilly Circus was blocked by tens of thousands of chanting fans, hippies and straights and heads and bobbies and fathers and mothers and there were no Beatles at all at the premiere at London Pavilion and it was bloody sad, bloody, bloody awful.

We were there, Neil and Mal and Peter and Derek and

our wives and friends, *their* friends, we were there. We felt miserable and guilty at sharing in something so innately untruthful, as celebrative as a premiere, for we knew that grim as the worst moments in the film may seem, the real facts and abstractions were terrible.

Speaking only for myself, and for the first time, it is now clear that working for the Beatles for too long had taken away from me not only what joining them had given me – an intense sense of being contemporary and wholly alive to the possibilities of life as it is lived moment by moment – but also what I had *always* had: a capacity for fun. I no longer enjoyed anything because I didn't believe I had the right to any more.

In the days after the premiere I dreaded one of them asking me: 'Did you go to the premiere?' I don't know whether Neil feared this, but I feel he feared it. I did not care to ask him about his fear, in case the answer was 'yes', for if he too had this, then I would know that what I had was not my paranoia alone, but an infection. If the Beatles were having no fun, then how dared we?

In truth, Apple's paranoia was an epidemic and anyone still in the building in Savile Row (supported physically by scaffolding and financially by the continuing massive earning power of their words and music, emotionally by nothing more soothing than the chatter of adding machines and whispered conversations) will tell you it is hard to be there nowadays.

How can things get to this state? I don't know the precise answer to that one. It seems, looking back, that maybe the good Apple times were hard times. When Apple was doing well (and contrary to anything you read or heard or imagined, all the Scotch everyone drank multiplied by 1,000, would not have been able to make any indentation on the huge income generated by the Beatles and their devoted staff) the press chipped away hoping to find decay, and if they found none, then they left enough trails of doubt and scorn to make everyone feel a little less easy with themselves.

I guess everything got too big, too bloody vast for human beings, frail, ill-prepared human beings, to cope, whether Beatles (and we had to concede it in the end, oh yes we did, they *were* human, should have realised *that* when Ringo had his tonsils out with the bidding at $10,000 for them), or us, nervous at their feet. We couldn't take it.

So . . . so . . . in the end, the love you take is equal to the love you make. We weren't making much love in the late sixties, not any of us. All the bold gold promises of heaven on earth for all artists everywhere, they went out the window by summer of 68 and by 1969 even Magic Alex was unmagicked. Came 1970 and even going to the pictures to see *Let It Be* was cause for guilt and shame? Christ!

The manner of the ending of the Beatles is a shame, a real bad bummer. Maybe one day it will seem easier, I trust so. But had they continued, they and all of us who gave them their fixes and got our own in return, we would not have survived to tell the tale.

I say now, it didn't end a day too soon.

24 / About the present and recent past – written 1970.
Do you like boxing?

_____

Monday, it came and went.

And then it was Tuesday, a new day, another day, and one less to guess about.

That afternoon, Dave Clark called me on the telephone and asked me if I liked boxing. He called me and said: 'Hi, this is Dave, Derek, Dave Clark, do you like . . .' and just as he was about to say 'boxing' I got a flash that he might be going to say 'do you like *me*' so that when he actually got out the word boxing, I already had my answer ready: 'Yes.' The answer was so pat and inaccurate, I blush. I had no chance to change it because I do like Dave Clark so much and he is so decent that even had he asked me, 'Do you like playing with a poodle's balls?' I should probably have answered 'yes'. I wouldn't want to confuse Dave by answering no to anything, just never would I say no to Dave.

So, I said yes I like boxing, and nothing is further from the truth, nothing. I think it is a terrible way of passing time. The only thing I can see in it is that for those who are strong enough, it is a way of earning a living. But, *watching* it, for fun? Oh no.

So I told Dave 'yes' and he said: 'That's good, so do I.' He said, 'I have a little party coming up. I'm a member of the National Sporting Club and every month we have a dinner at the Hilton Hotel and I would like you to come to this month's with me and Mike Smith and Dudley Moore and Bryan Forbes. It'll be young featherweights.' I said I would be delighted and Joan said afterwards that it must be 'business'; what else could it be that would bring Dave Clark, Bryan Forbes, Dudley Moore, Mike Smith and me together at the Hilton Hotel to watch young boys punching each other's heads.

Dave is a super host; he doesn't drink but he pours with immense generosity. He is cheerful and straight and he cares. He doesn't worry about the rights and wrongs of boxing any more than he cares about the rights and wrongs of fox hunting. But he does care about the rights and wrongs of the way his friends are treated and charity begins at home and I know a lot of people with social consciences on their sleeves and poison on their lips who don't care.

Not Dave Clark, man, oh no.

We went to the Hilton, Bryan Forbes, Dudley Moore, Dave Clark, Mike Smith and me. A very strange bunch of people, no stranger than our fellow guests. Lord Wigg is one of the guests on the top table; he was one of those who nailed Profumo on the wall. Lester Piggott is there. And Jimmy Tarbuck, Henry Cooper, many jockeys of horses and discs and enough agents and managers to fill the Old Bailey, which is where some of them belong.

During the evening, some little people dressed as jockeys take a collection and a procession of slim boys come into the ring to beat each other up. I had never known that blood was so pink. It was nasty to watch and, I'm sure, nastier still to be in the ring. Sitting around, drinking and watching and belching and picking their teeth the obese louche figures of show-business seemed delighted with it all.

Dave was not happy with the way the evening was going, I thought. He said: 'It's better when the heavyweights are fighting,' but he wasn't convincing. I think he meant that it would have been better if the spilled blood had been a little *older*, or from the veins of men with more to spare than these thin lads who seemed so frail, so young.

We were all relieved when someone began to auction racing relics. Lester Piggott's signed saddle was offered, I bid for it to £60 and won it. What the hell am I doing, I wondered aloud. 'What indeed?' said Dave, and talked the auctioneer out of it. They insisted on bringing me the saddle, and I think I pretended to be French, or foolish, and by not actually looking at them as they passed the stinking leather thing over the table, it was possible to view the whole affair as unreal and after all, what on earth was one doing there, with all these strange blood-spattered people bidding for signed saddles? Going crazy maybe?

There's no business like show-business like no business I know.

Invitations to dinner and boxing come to me rarely. All the more surprising then in 1968 when Nancy Sinatra got Ron Joy to call me in Hollywood to invite me over to her house for dinner and to watch some boxing movies.

(Ron Joy was Nancy's Misterright in those days – it was 1968 – and I knew him from the Beatle tour in 1964 when he was a photographer. Ron is all rogue, all Hollywood, all charm and good looks and he is a friend. He is always hustling a deal and he wears his shades on his head and his pants are very well cut. You won't catch Ron in a Mustang and he has a tan. Do you know him?)

The idea was that maybe I would write Nancy's autobiography, which would be the story of her life with her father and the thought of getting into that one was very fascinating. FRANK SINATRA? Wow. I had been to see Nancy earlier, at her office which was in the 9000 Building of horrid memory. She was still linked with Lee Hazelwood, Boots Productions, then, and she was a patriot.

The office was red and white and blue and crisp as can be. She was a most fetching hostess and she said the book would be called: *He Was a Very Gentle Man* and I figured that as Frank's daughter, she would have a view of him that was nothing to do with public image. 'So he is gentle?' I said to her and she said: 'As a baby!' 'No warts?' I said. 'None that I can see,' she said, and I believed her and I still do and I can't wait to read the book for, in the end, it was to be written by someone else so that's a good thing.

I told Ron I would like to come to dinner with them and watch boxing movies. Would Frank be there? No, said Ron. What's he like? A little strange, said Ron. That would be a great title for the book, I thought: *He Was a Very Gentle Man, But a Little Strange.*

The evening of the dinner party I walked from my office at A&M Records up Sunset Boulevard to the Gaiety Delicatessen where old Ben the Barman had just come on evening duty. Ben was Ben Stokes whom Joan and I had named godfather to Dominic our American child, but there was no christening or anything like that, just that over a drink we

208

had named Ben godfather and that was it. Good ole big Ben.

To get to Nancy's in the Hills I had to walk up the Strip to the Gaiety, passing on the way the Whisky à Go Go where John Powers used to stand in those times when we were all trying to catch the wind of the Monterey Pop Festival, now over, but still a joyous memory. John Powers, tall and ginger and sincere, had been in charge of transport for some of the festival. No one knew how or where he had come from but like many of the people at such events, he just was and that was enough. The festival over, he really had no place to go. Many of us didn't. There should be festivals all the time for such as John. Now he was trying to push books of psyche-delic drawings, not bad of their kind. He gave me one he had painted which hangs still in the bathroom downstairs. Also, he gave me four books for the Beatles, and one for myself which is the way people usually gave me things.

I asked John if he had his car handy, could he drive me to Bev Hills. He couldn't, but he could score me a cab, he said. He couldn't, but he tried.

It was an excuse to go to the Gaiety, I phoned a cab and Ben asked where was I going. I said I was going to see Nancy Sinatra. 'Good,' he said. 'That father sure done some living.' Right.

At the house they were all sitting down to dinner but they hadn't gone too far, maybe a course and a half. I was asked to sit at the head of the table. A fatherly figure, maybe an uncle. There were a few there I didn't know.

Samantha Eggar was on my left ('Where are you from?' she asked; us being British) and her husband was on her right and quite uptight. On my right was Guy McElwaine, a press

209

agent about to become a manager, a man about Hollywood, Guy, once represented lots of people till it went even sourer than usual. Ron Joy was there of course, plus a young guy who looked like he was the only pothead around, 'cept for me, and me, I took for granted.

Down table there were two heavy guys, older than the rest of us. I figured they had come for the movies. Nancy was very delightful, fussing over everything being right and it was. The movies were started and it turned out it was about two hours of knockouts, all the famous knockouts that had ever been filmed. Some blood and bashing to be sure; nothing but. The old guys slumped in their armchairs and gave themselves to the movies and I sat some way back. Nancy came over and sat down. 'Do you like boxing?' she asked, and this time I was able to say, no I didn't, it was very violent and upsetting. She said, 'I agree. I don't like it either.'

I never did ask why we were all there watching it. I guess there was a very good reason, but it must have been multi-level subtle. From somewhere, a guitar came out and the pothead sang and I wished I had a joint. Tom Stern, Samantha's husband came over and muttered that he would like to get high and that made three of us. But none of us had anything to smoke and the evening passed and we all went home, all except Nancy who was home all the time. Must be difficult being a Sinatra.

Difficult being Derek Taylor, though. Difficult being.

When we moved to America I got a lot of letters asking for a Derek Taylor Fan Club; did you ever *hear* of such a thing? I thought it would be fantastic to have a fan club, such a trip, to be the only press agent in the world with a fan club, you know, just for the sake of it and so on. Power without responsibility. It isn't like that, though. Isn't it? No it is not.

Out of the letters, all of them asking to be the one who started it, I picked the most businesslike; it was from a girl named Shelly Heber who lived in outer LA, someplace like that, and she got it all together with newsletters and photographs and Christmas cards and Joan was very worried about the enterprise. 'What do you want a fan club for?' she would ask and no answer was the stern reply. Shelly got a committee and twice they came to our house in Nichols Canyon, bearing gifts of food and records and books, including the *Judy Garland Story*, and album, and *Lenin's Life*, a book. They were very kind to me and all that, but it was becoming very inappropriate as far as I could see because, in truth, the girls were Beatle fans and it was really because of this that any of it got off the ground and when the time came for me to hold a convention of members in the 9000 Building to accept a huge gift and lecture them on 'The Beatles as People', I really got cold feet, typed letters of resignation, moved them express mail across the state and cancelled out the fan club for good and all and may God give me humility enough never to do such a thing again. I hope the girls are all married and happy now with good things to do.

25 / About the past forty years – written 1970.
Of heroes and villains

On meeting the great and famous of many lands.

One of the first Famous Men I ever had anything to do with was Dai Rees, who was also the first man I ever heard say of a game: 'I'm not doing this for the fun you know.'

That was at the Royal Liverpool Golf Club in the late forties and it explained a lot about games that I'd never understood. It certainly underlined why sport was taken so seriously at school. It's fashionable now to read about contemporary heroes who were no good at games, rugger-haters who used sick-notes and dead grandmothers and spontaneous limps to excuse themselves from the dreadful game, but in those days you never read stuff like that and only read about shitty worms and cowards lined up to be insulted by sado-masochistic gamesmasters on Wednesday afternoons. Oh it was fashionable for Churchill to boast of having failed at Harrow, but he failed at *work*, not at *play*.

Our reading in those days was like this, from the *Boy's Own Paper*, an extract from a morality story. 'The Day Boys' House', designed to support the then unfashionable view that day boys might, if they were good at rugger, be acceptable at boarding-school . . .

'Rather rot having to play the day boys,' said Merrit, the

captain. 'Still, we're safe for the final anyway.' 'Don't you be so cocksure!' retorted Baines. 'I have heard some yarn about them practising in town every night. Maybe you'll get a surprise packet.' And in truth it was.

Not only did D House fail to gain a place in the final, but they were ignominiously routed by their despised rivals. The fact that the day boys were putting up a team at all and the prospect of a little football of the comic order attracted a crowd of spectators. What they saw, however, filled them with astonishment and in some cases, consternation. This was not the collection of unskilled and untrained loafers they had expected, but a *team*.

The team of day boys went on, of course, to win and the story ended with the words: 'From that day forward there has never been any question at St Austin's as to whether they can play football in Day Boys' House.'

In context, and of its time, it was a well-intentioned story though there is no knowing how the day boys would have come off at school if they hadn't won at rugger. Badly, I guess. Very badly. And in our scene we were all day boys so it was difficult to relate to boarding-school anyway. What we cried for were stories like life. But there were none. Not one. There were stories about midgets who excelled at fly-half and skinny freaks who turned out to be good on the wing but I didn't ever find a story where the hero was the bony boy who smoked and stole and lied and cheated and, since our stories were our only escape from living our life, we were very short on reassurances, us smokers, thieves, liars and cheats.

However, folks, we pulled through and lived to see the day,

213

later though it is, when most of our heroes are as awful as we could never admit to being. Jesus, it took patience to wait so long, but it happened.

Back in the forties, heroes were very heavy. Dai Rees, when he said he wasn't playing golf for fun, didn't mean that he was playing so that he could be acceptable in society; what he meant was that he was playing for money, playing to win, and I didn't introduce him into this essay so that I could moralise about right and wrong, and winning and losing, but only to make the point that he was the first person I ever had anything to do with who was really famous. I got his *autograph*, through my father who played billiards with him at West Kirby Sailing Club. Billiards with a golfer at a *sailing* club?

My father also got me Sam King's autograph and he said I was lucky getting both Dai Rees's and Sam King's which was true enough but I didn't really dig Sam King's because he wasn't famous and there is something very freaky about having the autograph of someone you never heard of. I tried to give it some significance, like I would take my book to school and say, 'Look, I got Dai Rees's autograph *and* Sam King's' and they would say. 'Yeah? Who's Sam King?' I would say, he's the golfer, he's in all the golf books and they would say well we never heard of him but we heard of Dai Rees.

That was the beginning of what I grew to understand about stars, that there are stars and there aren't and there isn't really any disputing it by pointing out qualities or specifics or saying that Billy Bronze is a better guitarist than John Lennon but he didn't get the breaks. 'Who the hell cares, man, who cares? We never heard of Billy Bronze.' Billy Bronze is the golfer's guitarist. Billy Bronze is a star? Drop dead. Billy Bronze is a star, go fuck yourself man.

Next famous man I met was Elton Hayes, who sang to a Small Guitar in the 1940s. Met him at a press reception in Liverpool when I was working on the *Hoylake and West Kirby Advertiser* and we would get invitations to travel to the big city to meet with stars like Elton Hayes when movies were being launched in the provinces. Hayes was a nice little guy with a large head, like Matt Monro, and weighing it up a little later I concluded that the reason he was promoting the movie (*Robin Hood*, in which he played Alan-a-Dale, wandering troubadour who sang to a small guitar) was that Richard Todd, the real star, couldn't be bothered travelling to Liverpool from London, so that was another lesson I learned about stars and lesser stars who aren't.

Next contact I had with the Great was when Richard Attenborough came to visit his auntie who lived in West Kirby. I was about seventeen and I called his auntie and said this was the *Advertiser*, could I speak to Richard Attenborough? I was paralysed with fear; what could a Nobody like me say to a Man who had been in *In Which We Serve* with Noel Coward?

His auntie said Mr Attenborough had just gone for a drive and would probably call me later if he had time.

He was out! Thank God for that. And he was out driving in *our* village. Fancy a great actor like Richard Attenborough out like anyone else, driving and maybe, shopping!

Next thing was the phone rang and it was him. Like hell he was out driving. 'Good afternoon,' said a honeyed voice. 'This is Richard Attenborough. I understand a member of your staff wishes to talk to me.'

Richard Attenborough was on this telephone? Jesus, it would be Jean Simmons next! I don't know what we talked about and I don't have the clipping, but there's no doubt it was a very corny conversation and the lesson was that Richard Attenborough had the time to talk to the local press even if he was a big movie star, so why? Public relations or common courtesy. At seventeen, there was no doubt in my mind, Mr Attenborough was a gentleman.

Britain's all time biggest-ever star mania in those days centred on Danny Kaye, and when *he* came to Hoylake to play golf, the star chasing was tense. The girl reporter and me, we both ran like lunatics to borrow box cameras from Wilson's the Chemists.

'Now hold on,' said Big Bill Wilson, 'he takes just as long to play a round of golf as the next man. He's only a man like the rest of us. What's the hurry? He's only a man like the rest of us.'

Only a man like the rest of us?

Bill Wilson must be out of his mind. We took half the golf course each, the girl (Dorothy) and me, I never did catch up with him and the worst of it was that she did. One exposure, the only one of eight on the film to 'come out' was published the next week and, sure enough, it was Danny Kaye all right. I had hoped it would be Sam King or someone else no one had ever heard of.

About twenty years later, and twenty years too late, in mania terms, I did meet Danny Kaye, in Hollywood days. Warren Cowan the press agent called me at Herb Alpert's A&M and says will I have cocktails with him.

I say I will, in the La Brea Inn at La Brea and Sunset. We

play a lot of games with each other; he asks me where I'm at, like am I *really* thick with the Beatles, do they *respect* my opinion, and I ask him what's the pitch because I'm not very good at those questions. He tells me he is married to Barbara Rush and then he says he represents 'a very exceptional performer of whom you may have heard,' smirk . . . smirk . . . smirk . . . grin . . . grin . . . grin . . . wink . . . wink, 'A man named Danny Kaye.'

Oh *really*. *The* Danny Kaye. Warren looks nervous; is he being put on?

'No, Warren, I dig Danny Kaye very much. I once queued outside the Liverpool Empire for thirteen hours to buy a ticket for a Danny Kaye show, in 1949, Warren.' Warren is still doubtful, but he says, 'Danny is looking for a new, aaah,' (How shall he put it?) 'a new *direction*.' In short, as the Beatles are about to launch Apple, and as I know the Beatles and as I seem a bright sort of (young, yes?) guy, maybe I would care to visit with Danny and talk things over? 'Yes, Warren.'

Next day I drive to Danny Kaye's place in Fellatio Drive, Beverly Hills and Warren is there with a very nice nervous smiling Hollywood cat who says he is Herb Bonis and he looks after things for Mr Kaye, if I should ever want anything, here is his number, which he writes on the cover of a *Sgt Pepper* album I just happen to have with me.

About two minutes later Danny walks in and says 'Hi'. He looks me over and he looks me up and he looks me down and he turns to Warren and he says: 'He doesn't look like a kook to me, Warren, he looks OK.' Warren would have squirmed if, to survive under his chosen stone, he hadn't had to forget how. He merely says: 'Oh, now Danny, come

217

on.' 'Thanks a lot, Warren,' I say. 'Like, who was it asked me up here?' Danny is very nice and seems very stoned. I ask him would he like some grass and he shakes his head. Anyway, Warren has told him I was a fan and queued up and that pleases him and Warren splits and Danny plays me and Bonis some 78s and after a couple of hours I split and say he should record 'Fool on the Hill' which I will drop in next day, and I do and he doesn't record it, or anything else which is probably a pity and like Bill said, Danny Kaye is no different from the next man and there was no hurry to run up the Royal Liverpool Golf Course or anywhere else. A shame Warren Cowan couldn't have met Bill Wilson because Warren and all those press agents are still running to keep up with the famous and it is a bum trip because the pace is too fast for just everyone. The famous, the rich, they are just people, like all the rest of us.

Though it took years and years and years, I destroyed the lunatic part of stargazing and the dimensions arranged themselves until it was clear as the noses that the great and the ungreat all have on their mortal, decaying faces, that the great and the ungreat are all One People under God, only some are on television and others aren't. Did it have to take so long to find out? I dunno.

Yet I didn't really find out for real, because though I knew the Beatles were human, I looked at them as leaders and together with everyone else who had grown to love them, I began to build the legend of invincibility and together with everyone else who *knew*, knew for sure, that Dylan was right about parking meters, I looked to the Beatles to show the way and the poor devils were themselves crying out in pain and in vain that they were looking for a Way, a Truth and a Life, and not finding it.

John through Yoko and Peace, Paul and Ringo through familial cosiness, George through Krishna, all searching . . . all of them just like the next man . . . and when I discovered that, I was, again, alone. You too?

26 / Endpeace

In the early summer of 1973 Allen Klein split from Apple and from the three Beatles who had accepted him as their friend and guide and here and there were heard joyful sounds, not all of them muted. There were varying stories about how and why the parting happened. Klein said he made the break, the others say they did. Whatever . . . it didn't work out and there will be a lot of howsyerfather hitting the fan before you can say Jack Lawsuit and as someone once said the writs will be as thick as the Watergate files.

News of the split brought a terrific cry of relief from Paul and Linda McCartney who had in any case become much closer with George, John and Ringo. Things move fast in these circles that it is very likely they all will have appeared on the same stage (though not as Beatles for that was the sixties) by the time you read this.

Already, Richard Perry, the record producer who has done so much to help other distinguished artists, has acted as catalyst by producing much work involving all four former Beatles (though, again, not all at the same time) and it is indeed good news that all good things can carry on and not end with whimpers and counter-accusations and nasty outbursts in the unpopular press.

What else has happened? George made a fine new album

and Ringo another, John another and Paul another, all with a little help from their friends. Ringo made three movies: one with Harry Nilsson (my genius friend for whom I produced an album this year), Harry playing Dracula, Ringo, Merlin; another with Marc Bolan; another with David Essex. All three are fine vehicles for a lovely man. George and Pattie continue to thrive . . . all the marriages are intact, their children prosper and grow as do mine. Joan is a liberationist and I give her my love, encouragement and support.

Finally, thank you Norma Whittaker for research, and to all the thousands who have helped to make the book possible, thanks and goodnight for now.

Index

223

225